# Skiing & snowboarding

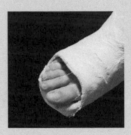

# Skiing and snowboarding

52 brilliant ideas for fun on the slopes

## Cathy Struthers

brilliantideas

## CAREFUL NOW

As you may have gathered from some of the chapter titles in this book – 'Avalanche!', 'Get ready to tumble', 'Bouncing back from injury' – snowsports aren't exactly risk free. And while the risk attached to any form of adventure sport is what gets the buzz of adrenaline coursing through any true snow junkie's veins, I am obliged to point out that that risk is yours, not ours. Yes, this is the waiver part.

If you're cool enough to make snowsports part of your life you're also cool enough to use your head. So don't bow to peer pressure, or ignore your intuition and ride where you don't feel safe – no run is worth dying for. Don't forget to gear up properly. Helmets have street cred these days, so wear one. And don't explore off-piste with just anyone – employ the services of a qualified guide or heli-skiing outfit.

Unfortunately in our mollycoddled, risk-averse 21st century I have to tell you that neither the author nor the publisher can be held responsible or liable for any loss or claim arising out of the use, or misuse, of the suggestions made in this book. So, if you aren't sure whether your body is up to all those pre-ski exercises, the après-ski or the actual on-piste action, take advice from your doctor first.

First published in 2006 by
**The Infinite Ideas Company Limited**
36 St Giles
Oxford, OX1 3LD
United Kingdom
www.infideas.com

A CIP catalogue record for this book is available from the British Library

ISBN 1-904902-51-0

Brand and product names are trademarks or registered trademarks of their respective owners.

Designed by Baseline Arts Ltd, Oxford
Typeset by Sparks, Oxford
Printed by TJ International, Cornwall

# Brilliant ideas

# Brilliant features

**Each chapter of this book is designed to provide you with an inspirational idea that you can read quickly and put into practice straight away.**

Throughout you'll find four features that will help you get right to the heart of the idea:

- *Here's an idea for you ...* Take it on board and give it a go – right here, right now. Get an idea of how well you're doing so far.

- *Try another idea ...* If this idea looks like a life-changer then there's no time to lose. *Try another idea ...* will point you straight to a related tip to enhance and expand on the first.

- *Defining idea ...* Words of wisdom from masters and mistresses of the art, plus some interesting hangers-on.

- *How did it go?* If at first you do succeed, try to hide your amazement. If, on the other hand, you don't, then this is where you'll find a Q and A that highlights common problems and how to get over them.

# Introduction

**Eighteen years ago, dressed in a fetching neon pink all-in-one, I stepped onto skis for the first time. Six years later I started sliding sideways on a snowboard. And so began a lifelong love affair with the white stuff.**

Hooked on the winter, I started writing for snowsports and travel magazines and spending all my hard-earned chasing the snow. Like many of the snowsports junkies I know, I haven't had a summer beach holiday in years.

Whether you're in it for the adrenaline buzz, the social scene or the tremendous feeling of freedom it brings, this book is for you. Mimicking snowsports themselves, 52 Brilliant Ideas embraces freedom, fluidity and inspiration.

Why would you cruise straight down a piste from top to bottom when you could be mixing it up in powder stashes, hitting natural jumps and bobbing through the trees at the side? In the same way, why read a book from start to finish when you could leap from idea to idea as new thoughts hit you and inspiration carries you?

That's the concept of this book – a veritable off-piste playground of ideas, tips and advice that you can dip into and apply straight away.

This is also one of the first books that speaks to both skiers and snowboarders. Why? We believe that one plank/two plank divide is well and truly a thing of the past.

With the exception of the stubborn few resorts which still insist on banning snow-boarders from their slopes, skiers and snowboarders have found a new synergy between their sports.

These days snow junkies carve on skis one day then jump on their board the next. Skiing has been given a new breath of life by tapping into snowboard style. The two sports have never shared so much – competitions, terrain, tricks, clothes, style – each sport borrows from and shares with the other.

Dumped down with powder overnight? Grab your snowboard and make the most of its large surface area and float your way down the mountain. Too icy for one edge? Slip your skis on and make the most of that extra plank for some high speed carving.

With this in mind, we've set out to arm you with an avalanche of inspirational ideas, practical advice and insider tips on how to make the most out of your all-important time on the snow. Whether you're on one plank or two, it doesn't matter. It's about making your bucks stretch further, making your body ski harder and making the fun last longer.

Unless you're one of the lucky few who call the mountains their office, your time at altitude is limited and this book will help you squeeze the most out of every moment up there. Before you go, you'll learn how to buy the best kit, how to pick the best destination for you and how to hone and tone your body for the slopes. Once you're there you can dip into technique tips, sports psychology to psych yourself up for the steeps and all-important survival advice for venturing further afield. And, you'll even get inspiration for what happens after your day on the slopes, with hangover health tips, ideas for helping your hardware last longer and trendsetting tips for what to look out for next time you head for the mountains.

But, as with all the best things in life, there's a price to be paid. In return for the feeling of freedom, the buzz of descent and being surrounded by the beauty of the mountains, you've got to deal with risk. As with any adrenaline sport, the risks can be high, but for many the inherent risk is a large part of the attraction.

If you don't fancy dicing with death just to get your adrenaline fix, don't worry, we've got it covered. We've got ideas, tips and no-messing advice on how to flatten fear, how to ride safely out of bounds and what to do in an emergency. Once you're done with this book, you'll be one of the safest people to ride with – everyone will want to be your ski buddy.

Once you've had your first taste of sliding on the white stuff, once you've experienced your first bluebird, powder day, once you've felt the freedom of flying, I guarantee you'll be hooked for good. For some, skiing and snowboarding are just a pleasurable way to work out, for others they're close to spiritual, but for most they are the purest form of fun. Grin fodder.

We want you to finish every day on the slopes as the best days should end ... with a beer in your hand, a tired body and a huge smile on your face as the last whisper of sunlight dances on the mountain peaks.

There's no doubt about it, a love affair with snowsports takes work ... but it could just be one of the most satisfying relationships you'll ever have.

*Cathy Struthers*

# 1

# Picking your planks

**So you're officially hooked on cruising the white stuff. But when's the right time to turn your back on rental shop queues and buy your own pair of skis? And where on earth do you start? Fret not, help is at hand.**

Buying your first pair of skis is a scary step. With more models than ever — fat, shaped, straight — it can be a bewildering experience. Let us guide you.

When faced with the prospect of parting with a wodge of cash, usually around credit-munching Christmas, the lesser financial dent of hiring skis is often easier to stomach. But, if you intend to head to the mountains year after year, it will almost certainly be cheaper to buy in the long run.

There's nothing worse than arriving in a resort, supercharged for the slopes, and having to spend your first precious hours hanging around in queues at the hire shop. Being able to shun the stress of ski fittings for the uncrowded slopes of changeover day has to be one of the best reasons for splashing out on your own pair of planks.

Thankfully technology has reached a point where there are no such things as bad skis on the market and you can get a good pair without having to spend too much.

## SO WHERE DO YOU START?

Get advice from a specialist outdoor retailer who can advise what type of ski will suit you. But be sure to ask shop staff if they have actually skied on the ski. If they say no, pick another shop with experienced staff who know their stuff.

Gone are the days when the longer your skis, the better skier you were expected to be, which means no more testosterone-fuelled competition to get two metre skis. Generally speaking a pair of intermediate skis should come up to your nose and not be too stiff.

*Here's an idea for you...*

**Sit down and make a list of everything you're looking for in a pair of skis. What level are you at now? What terrain do you want to be riding this time next year? What do you find especially challenging? What was the brand of your favourite pair of hire skis? Take your resulting wish list to the shop and you'll have far more chance of meeting your perfect match.**

Your skiing style is more important for determining which skis suit you, so be sure to inform shop staff of your style and aspirations. If you're happy to cruise around intermediate slopes you'll need a different ski than someone who aspires to double black diamonds.

## HOW CAN I SAVE?

End of season sales are a good way to get a brand new pair of skis at a good price. If you buy abroad, in a ski resort, you can often 'try before you buy', although this service is often reserved for experienced riders buying high end skis.

The main drawback with buying abroad is that you have few guarantees if the skis are wrong for you or if anything breaks.

Instead, hunt out local retailers offering a demo service on upper end skis, where you can take the skis either abroad or to a local ski hill or dry slope. This service usually costs, but if you end up buying the skis you'll get the price of the demo rental knocked off.

**Don't forget your boots. Comfy boots can make or break your skiing day (who hasn't blamed a bad day's skiing on cramp, blisters or numb toes?). Turn to Idea 30,** *Keep your feet sweet***, for the low-down on what to look for.**

*Try another idea…*

If you know what you are looking for and understand ski tech, then you're a prime candidate for buying second-hand. Like buying a second-hand car, it's easy to end up with a duff one if you're not sure what you're looking for, so either take an expert with you or get some good advice first. Ebay, sales in shops and web chat rooms are good places to browse.

Stay a million miles away from long, narrow, old skis. Look for obvious damage to the base of the ski – sometimes the damage is hard to see; for example, when the base has been ground down a lot. And look out for impact damage like large dents.

**'Everybody's in good shape. Everybody knows how to ski. Everybody has good equipment. When it really boils down to it, it's who wants it the most, and who's the most confident in his skis.'**

REGGIE CRIST

*Defining idea…*

3

Ex-demo skis can also be good value if not over-used and if they have been regularly serviced.

If you plump for a spanking new pair, ask the shop to fit the bindings for you and make sure they are at a setting to suit your standard. Bindings tend to be integrated these days anyway, which makes for a lot less choice and a less confusing virgin purchasing experience.

*How did it go?*

**Q**   **I'm a tech head, so have decided to hire so that I can thrash the very latest skis every season – brainwave, eh?**

*A*   *If you're a good skier and know what you want, yes, it makes sense. Most shops in top resorts will rent out new VIP skis for a week for about a quarter of the price of buying them. If you do this, you can change them to suit snow conditions (swapping powder skis for carvers, for example). But, if you're at the beginner end of intermediate (and it's worth being honest with yourself), you're likely to get pot luck and end up with whichever brand the ski shop has bought in bulk at a good price. Rental skis, whatever your level, quickly get very worn ... you have been warned.*

**Q**   **The sales assistant seemed to know less than I did; does that really matter if all skis are so good now anyway?**

*A*   *Yes! Although it's hard to find a bad ski these days, you need to find one that's right for you. Switch to another retailer and shop around for the best advice.*

# 2

# Find your feet

**Want to ski better, faster, longer, without doing a shred of technique work? Then it's time to get aligned.**

There is always something to blame after a mediocre day's skiing — numb feet, dodgy knees, uncomfortable boots.

No matter how perfect you think your posture is, it's highly unlikely you are perfectly aligned. Whether it's a foot that rolls inward or quads that are stronger than your hamstrings, poor alignment is a lot more common than you might think.

Usually people progress quickly the first three times they go skiing or boarding, and then they begin to plateau. If this sounds like you, the reason could simply be poor alignment – your joints and centre of gravity may not be evenly balanced for maximum stability and strength. Because of this, you're effectively fighting yourself the whole time.

Picture a boot as a lever that controls the ski or snowboard and it isn't hard to see that any weakness or imbalance will have dire consequences on performance. Although the body has an amazing ability to compensate, if you suffer sore knees, hips and lower back while skiing; if you tire easily or experience a lack of ski control, the chances are you'll benefit from an alignment or biomechanics assessment.

Here's an idea for you...

**Get your snowboard stance right by standing relaxed on board and feeling for a comfortable width between your legs. You should be able to easily stand with your weight on one foot or the other without having to move very much at all. Now bend your knees. They should now be in line with your feet, over your toes. Note the angle difference between your feet. Now put your rear foot close to zero before putting the same angle as before back into your stance by adjusting the front foot. When you flex, your knees should comfortably flex over your feet as before.**

Few of us have perfect alignment. Most have either muscle imbalances (caused by tight muscles) or skeletal imbalances that can lead to knock knees and bow legs.

Skiers are particularly affected because muscular and skeletal imbalances influence how well skis sit on the snow (on a snowboard 'correct' alignment isn't possible because your feet aren't set dead straight, but at angles). If you're a knock-kneed skier, for example, you'll have both inside edges engaged even when gliding, making it hard to initiate and complete turns. If you're a bit bow-legged, you'll get the opposite effect and little chance of decent edge grip.

Other common problems relate to foot motion. About 70 – 80% of feet roll inwards (pronate), while others roll outwards (supinate). Skiers who pronate tend to find that the knee and hip collapse towards the inside of the skis, creating too much pressure on the inside edges towards the front of the ski. A foot that supinates has the opposite effect. Both put you at increased risk of knee injuries.

## ASSESSMENT A GOOD IDEA

Typically an assessment begins with an analysis of how your foot functions and how that affects your posture. Most assessments will also measure your weight distribution on a scientific pressure mat. If your weight is too far back, on the heel, you put huge strain on the quadriceps. Too far forward and you stress the calf muscles.

If you have muscle imbalances, a stretching programme may help realign you. Otherwise, custom-moulded insoles or orthotics give the support needed to harmonise your body with your equipment.

## SNOWBOARD SET-UP

For snowboarders whose pins rarely sit parallel anyway, it's more about watching your stance set-up. Ever since Terje Haakonsen started sweeping up in competitions across the globe, riders have been trying to emulate his style by copying his stance. As a result, 'duck' – where you ride with both feet turned outwards – has never been so popular. But how healthy is it?

Well, it's good for rotations in the air and for easier landing to ride fakie. But for all-mountain riding, it is too limiting. You need rotation around the hips to allow you to face more down the hill, rather than directly sideways, and this is what duck limits. This limitation of movement can place huge torsion strain on the body. With your hips unable to twist, the rotational forces affect the knees.

**Turn to Idea 30, *Keep your feet sweet*, and find out how to choose the perfect pair of boots to boost your riding.**

Try another idea…

**'Efficiency is intelligent laziness.'**
DAVID DUNHAM

Defining idea…

The knee joint allows flexion and extension in one direction (forwards and back-wards), so applying an additional strain at the knee can cause problems.

Ideally, your hips need to be slightly off-axis along the board to allow for this so you need a greater 'toe out' on the leading foot.

How did it go?

**Q** **Horrible! I had my assessment, made the adjustments and had an insole fitted, but it just feels terrible and I've lost the ability to ski – why?**

*A* *Don't worry! Although your first realigned outing on snow may feel odd, it should only take a couple of runs to adjust. It will provide you the freedom to perform skills that you have never be able to do before. If done correctly, it will release the handbrake from your skiing. So get back out there and persevere.*

**Q** **I find it hard work to ride on my heel side edge on a snowboard – can re-alignment help?**

*A* *It's probably as simple as adjusting your binding. Try putting more forward lean on your high back. It needs to be angled forwards so that you can feel it behind your calves and easily push your board onto the heel edge without having to pull up on your toes too much, or to straighten your legs.*

# 3

# Wanna get high?

**The world's highest resorts may deliver if you're after steep and deep, but being on top of the world doesn't necessarily mean you'll feel it. It's time to get clued up for high altitude health.**

If altitude sickness conjures up images of hard core mountain men scaling the peaks of Everest, think again. Because if you're off to Colorado, Utah, Chamonix or one of the many high elevation ski resorts this winter, it could be you taking centre stage.

Here's the classic scenario: You fly to Denver at 1525m (5000ft). You pick up your hire car and drive straight up to Aspen at 2422m (7945ft). Eager to squeeze in a quick run to stave off jetlag, you take the cable car to the summit at 3418m (11,212ft). Then, as you stop off in the mountain restaurant, it hits you. Your head starts to pound, you feel sick and dizzy. You (and 30% of other visitors to Colorado) have got acute mountain sickness (AMS).

*Here's an idea for you...* **Allow adequate time for acclimatisation. If you're headed for a high altitude resort (over 8000ft), try and arrange to spend a night at an intermediate elevation on your transfer out. If you're flying long haul, book into a hotel near your destination airport – that way you can sleep off jet lag, acclimatise and arrive the next day in tip top condition for cruising.**

Mountain experts reckon that about 20%–30% of people in ski areas between 2440m (8000ft) and 3048m (10,000ft) fall sick with AMS. If that figure seems high, it simply reflects what happens when people fly from essentially sea level to 2440m and then exercise vigorously straight away.

At the very least AMS is extremely unpleasant; typical symptoms include nausea, vomiting and a headache caused by your body failing to acclimatise to the decreased oxygen (hypoxia) as you go higher. At any moment there is an 'ideal' altitude where your body is in balance, usually the last height you slept at. Above this is an indefinite grey zone where your body can tolerate the lower oxygen levels, but to which you are not quite acclimatised. If you get above the upper limit of this zone, there is not enough oxygen for your body to function properly and these symptoms of hypoxic stress occur. Go too high and you get AMS, unpleasant and potentially fatal if you develop the worst-case scenario of high altitude pulmonary oedema (HAPO), when pulmonary circulation is constricted and fluid leaks from the blood vessels of the lungs.

### AM I AT RISK?

If you're seriously overweight, then yes. Research, published in the *Annals of Internal Medicine* suggests that obese people (with a body mass index (BMI) over 30) are at higher risk. The study was only small but symptoms were more severe in the obese participants, leading scientists to conclude that AMS may be closely related to increased body weight.

But generally the 'at risk' profile remains elusive. There is no convincing evidence that any group is much more susceptible than another and it's largely down to genetics. There may be a slightly increased risk for middle-aged men, but so far the boffins don't know why.

**Now your body is prepared for the effects of getting high, wise up to the effects of high altitude living on your skin. Turn to Idea 13, *Skin saviours*, to discover the secrets of flawless winter skin.**

*Try another idea...*

The only sure-fire treatment for AMS is to go lower. That's probably the last thing you want to do after your shuttle into resort, but it'll be worth it. Most moderate cases will disappear if you simply go no higher and rest. AMS will resolve as you acclimatise, generally in about one or two days. If you suspect you have an AMS headache take paracetamol, aspirin or Ibuprofen.

If you experience any symptoms of more severe altitude sickness, such as breathlessness, heart palpitations, blue-tinged skin and nails, or frothy, pink sputum (yep, as nasty as it sounds), seek medical attention immediately.

But prevention is better than cure so, if you know you repeatedly get ill at high altitude, ask your doctor about the drugs acetazolamide and dexamethasone which speed up acclimatisation. Other top tips? Avoid overexertion (on the piste and on the après-ski) on your first few days.

*'Life is brought down to the basics: if you are warm, regular, healthy, not thirsty or hungry, then you are not on a mountain. Being at altitude is like hitting your head against a brick wall – it's great when you stop.'*
CHRIS DARWIN, *The Social Climbers*

*Defining idea...*

13

*How did it go?*

**Q    I've experienced mild altitude sickness before and took drugs. Is there a natural alternative that can help?**

A    *If you don't fancy a trip to the doc to stave off AMS, recent studies suggest the herbal extract ginkgo biloba may be effective. Take 80–120mg twice a day starting five days before ascent and continuing at altitude. Keeping yourself well hydrated (with water, not the local tipple) is also a wise move.*

**Q    I avoided alcohol, I spent a day acclimatising, but after my first day shredding the slopes a classic AMS headache hit – what went wrong?**

A    *A bit of a weekend warrior are you? If you do scant exercise throughout the year and then overexert yourself on your first day in the white stuff, you may find yourself at greater risk of feeling the effects of altitude. If your BMI is over 25, you may also be at slightly increased risk. (To calculate your BMI, divide your weight in kilos by your height (in metres) squared or, if maths ain't your strong point, use the BBC's calculator, at www.bbc. co.uk/health/yourweight/bmi.shtml. Under 18.5 is considered underweight, over 25 is overweight, and over 30 is obese.)*

    *The solution? Avoid pushing yourself too hard on the first day – stick to the blue runs, a long lunch and an early night. You've got all week to party!*

# 4

# Cheap thrills

**A ski or snowboard holiday doesn't have to break the bank. Picking the right destination and being canny with booking it means that even the most Scrooge-like skier can get their kicks for less.**

*Don't worry, you don't have to live out of a VW camper van and work as a liftie to ski or snowboard cheaply. Get canny and you can ski on a shoestring.*

The cheapest ski holiday I've ever had wasn't the one that involved an 18-hour coach journey to get there, nor was it the one where I slept on the living-room floor with five other people. No, my cheapest winter trip yet was spent in a top-notch chalet with plasma screen TV, games room (complete with bar) and a hot tub on the deck.

How? I obeyed the golden rule of snowsports' Scrooges: plan your trip around everyone else's.

**Mountain cafés are notoriously expensive, so skip the overpriced hot dog and fries at resort restaurants. Instead, eat a hearty (preferably all-inclusive) breakfast before you get to the hill and take a packed lunch. It will make a huge difference to your pocket.**

## CHOOSE YOUR TIME ...

Finding good deals is always a matter of when you go. If you want to find rock-bottom prices, you need to be flexible with your timing. If you're a teacher, or have to plan your holiday around school breaks, sorry. There are other ways to do it on the cheap, but avoiding peak times has to be the most effective.

Christmas is almost always the most expensive time to ski or snowboard, with prices rising a whopping 30% or more from standard high season prices (high season is normally February and March, with prices to match, too).

You'll find the best deals in early December when everyone else is preoccupied with Christmas, and in early January, when they're feeling the pinch. Spring to late March and April – and even May in some resorts – is another cheap time to go and prices should dip by 20–40%.

The problem is that low season is 'low' for a reason – and generally that's because the snow is less reliable. In Europe, early December can be a tricky time, with most resorts not getting much until Christmas. Keep an eye on the forecast and hold off until the last minute to book.

January is usually more reliable and, as long as you don't mind very cold conditions, you can get some great conditions anywhere in the northern hemisphere.

Springtime is more of a hit and miss affair. You stand a good chance of epic conditions, but if it's too warm you may be short on snow. Again, hold off booking until late if you can, and target resorts that had particularly good winters.

Is budget the only thing you have to consider? Match your wish list to your resort in Idea 41, *Perfect match*.

*Try another idea…*

## … AND PICK YOUR SPOT

The second key price buster is picking the right resort. Lift tickets are always one of the most expensive parts of a ski trip and low-key resorts will always have cheaper passes than the big names. Try to pick resorts that are less well known or slightly off the beaten track. Many of the famous North American resorts, such as Jackson Hole, Vail, Heavenly and Banff, have smaller ski hills within a 30 minute drive away, which means you can still ski the big boys while staying somewhere for half the price. In Europe, try Ste Foy in the shadow of Tignes and Val d'Isère, or Brides-Les-Bains near the pricier Trois Vallées.

If you can also pick a resort that is busier as a summer destination (such as Banff or Jackson Hole), you'll benefit from cheaper 'low season' hotel rates. And if you can stand the thought of the daily ski shuttle bus, pick a hotel that's just outside the main resort where prices will sink even lower (generally around 20% lower). The shuttle bus is usually free and you'll probably find that restaurants, bars and shops just out of town will be far cheaper too.

No matter how independent a traveller you are, it's worth considering a snowsports

*'My problem lies in reconciling my gross habits with my net income.'*
Every skier or snowboarder can relate to ERROL FLYNN's problem.

*Defining idea…*

17

package since they are almost always cheaper and can often get you additional deals on car hire, lift passes and other activities. Again, timing comes into it. The best deals are most likely to be up for grabs if you book very early or very late.

How did it go?

**Q I got a great deal out here, but the expensive lift pass has put me way over budget. Any way I can save next time?**

*A If you don't snap up a lift pass through a package, buy one before you go via your resort's website where they will be cheaper than buying on the hill. If you don't think you can ski a full eight hours every day, or want to party hard and lie in, opt for a half-day ticket, which is typically at least 25% cheaper.*

**Q Where are the best budget destinations in Europe?**

*A The budget airlines' relentless expansion to the east means that Eastern Europe is an ever more attractive option for European snow junkies. Not only do the 'no frills' airlines make it dirt cheap to travel, but once you're actually there everything will be a fraction of the cost of not only the notorious ski resort norm but also your local high street. Cheap destinations include Andorra, Bulgaria, Slovenia (the biggest resort is Mariborsko Pohorje, with 80km of pistes) and Serbia.*

*To make your dosh stretch even further, watch the exchange rate before you go and opt for where your money is strongest.*

# 5

# The Vallée Blanche

**The Vallée Blanche is probably the most famous ski run in the world. Plunging down from the Aiguille du Midi at 3880m to Chamonix at 1100m, Europe's longest, most spectacular run is in a league of its own.**

Conquer the world's most famous off-piste run and your reward will be some of the most spectacular mountain scenery in the world, bragging rights and a grin you won't be able to wipe for days.

The statistics speak for themselves: A 22km (13½m) run with a mind-boggling 2780m (9120ft) vertical drop and a 30° ice ridge to boot. Gulp. It may sound extreme, but if you're a good intermediate you *can* do it.

Despite a quake-in-your-crampons start, the Vallée Blanche is not the most demanding skiing on the planet. In fact, any good intermediate can manage it. Above all you need to be consistent, with a good strong snowplough and good sideslip control. There are places where you need to weave your way between crevasses, but solid basic skills are all you need.

**Avoid the busy car park at the foot of the Aiguille du Midi cable-car, in Chamonix Sud. Instead, park your car in the Les Planards car park and walk back. After your run, you can then ski all the way back to town to the Planard slopes saving you a tiresome trek across town in ski boots when you're all skied out. If it's late season and you have to come down in the train, leave your car near the Montenvers glacier train station.**

The adventure starts at the base of the Aiguille du Midi cable car. If you're riding with a guide (which, unless you are a seriously experienced skier, you must), they should bring all the off-piste paraphernalia for you.

As well as an avalanche transceiver, you'll probably be given a climbing harness (it's easier to airlift you out if you're wearing one), a rope (to get you down the first ridge) and, if it's an icy day, crampons. If the butterflies kick in, don't worry. Although ice axes, harnesses and ropes will be part of your world for the next four hours, you don't need to turn into a hard core mountain man – you just get to wear all the gear.

## WHAT TO EXPECT

Emerging from the Aiguille du Midi cable-car at 3880m (12,730ft), the thin air will hit you immediately. The altitude can make you feel dizzy, so take time to adjust (don't try the Vallée Blanche on the first day of your holiday as your body won't have had the chance to acclimatise).

There are many different routes down, but the route most 'just for fun' riders take is the classic or 'vrai' Vallée Blanche. Just because it's the easiest route down, it doesn't mean you get to escape the notorious climb down a knife-edge ridge, or arête, from the top station of the cable-car.

Unless you get a kick out of scaring yourself silly, you'll want this bit over as quickly as possible. On one side, it's a 2700m (8860ft) vertical drop to Chamonix; on the other a 50° snow slope onto rocks. The path itself is about 30° with fixed ropes, and you'll probably be roped together with your group for safety, as the surface can be variable.

**Brush up on your off-piste safety skills before you hit the Vallée Blanche. Turn to Idea 33, *Piste off*.**

*Try another idea…*

At the bottom of the arête, you reap your reward – a couple of hours of continuous cruisy skiing through some of the most spectacular mountain scenery in Europe.

But don't relax too much. You need to stay in control to avoid the icy crevasses that litter the way. If you're on a snowboard, keep your speed up as you approach the 7km long Mer de Glace, which flattens out briefly. The area is huge and, despite the vast numbers of skiers and snowboarders who ride it every day, you will always be able to find untracked powder.

Beyond the flats of the Mer de Glace, boulders start to pepper the slopes and the glacial moraine and Chamonix below comes into view. You're home, having conquered the immense Vallée Blanche. Now go get bragging.

*'Mont-Blanc and the Valley of Chamonix, and the sea of Ice, and all the wonders of the most wonderful place are above and beyond one's wildest expectation. I cannot imagine anything in nature more stupendous or sublime.'*
CHARLES DICKENS, 1846

*Defining idea…*

**How did it go?**

**Q**  **All the guides are booked up. I've done a bit of off-piste before and surely there are enough people up there to make it safe enough to ski the Vallée Blanche without one?**

**A**  *Never ski the Vallée Blanche without a guide unless you are a seriously experienced backcountry skier. The Aiguille du Midi is not the place to find out how little you know. With the right gear and a good guide, your Vallée Blanche experience will be worry-free. On your own and poorly prepared, a minor mishap can very quickly land you in serious trouble.*

*Finding a guide in Chamonix is easy – all have passed the rigorous six-year Ecole Nationale du Ski Alpine and almost every local can recommend one.*

**Q**  **I spent ages in a queue for the lift and by the time I got to the top it was cloudy. When's the best time to ride the Vallée Blanche?**

**A**  *It's open any time between December and May, but try to avoid the early season though, as you'll be lucky to get a sunny enough day without wind. It's worth avoiding the tail end of the season as you won't be able to ski all the way down to Chamonix, and will have to take the Montenvers train down from around 2000m. When you do go, get up early to avoid the queues and make the most of clear skies. The lift opens at 7.30 a.m., but queues will already be stacking back by 9 a.m.*

*If you want to guarantee to beat the queues, ride the last cable-car of the day and stay overnight in the Cosmiques Refuge. The views are spectacular, but if you haven't acclimatised to the altitude, you won't get a good night's sleep.*

# 6

# Back on blacks

**It's a rare skier who hasn't experienced back pain – 85% of us will suffer at some stage – but it doesn't have to limit your fun on the hill.**

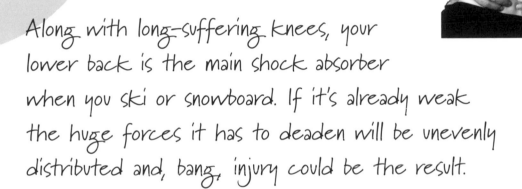

Along with long-suffering knees, your lower back is the main shock absorber when you ski or snowboard. If it's already weak the huge forces it has to deaden will be unevenly distributed and, bang, injury could be the result.

If you already get twinges of back pain, then sorry, but taking to skis is more than likely to aggravate it. The good news, however, is that over 90% of back pain is caused by muscle weakness, restricted joint movements or trapped nerves (rather than disease, tumours, fractures or disc damage) and responds well to treatment.

## WHAT TO DO ABOUT IT

If you're lucky, gentle activity may be all you need to alleviate your pain. Serious cases may need surgery (although nine out of ten back pain patients recover without it). But, for the bulk of back pain sufferers, plumping for one of the myriad

*Here's an idea for you...* **Try these exercises to strengthen your core supporting muscles so that you can adapt to the stresses you place on your spine. Sit on top of a Swiss ball and allow yourself to gently roll forward to move weight more onto your feet and so you feel your thigh muscles begin to contract. Slowly lift each leg alternately and hold for a few seconds. Next, on hands and knees balance on the ball for as long as you can, keeping a straight back. If you feel pain at any time, stop and seek further advice.**

of alternative treatments on offer could be the safest, fastest route to pain-free piste bashing.

Acupuncture is recommended by the British Medical Association as an effective way to treat back pain, and works by encouraging the body to heal itself. Needles are inserted into channels of 'Qi' (energy paths in the body) to stimulate the healing response. 'The effect can be dramatic,' says acupuncturist Wendy Longworth. 'If you've responded to acupuncture for something else before, it will almost certainly work for your back pain too, stimulating feel-good endorphins and serotonin, relaxing muscles and healing soft tissue.'

If you have acute back pain, a study by the Institute of Acupuncturists showed that it takes an average of 3.5 treatments to recover, while chronic sufferers usually need one further treatment.

Another tried and tested back remedy is osteopathy. Based on the theory that pain stems from abnormalities in body structure, as well as damage caused by disease, osteopathy takes a whole body view. 'Osteopathy seeks to find areas of restriction in the joints, muscles and tissue surrounding the muscles (fascia) and free them up,' says registered osteopath Jeremy Feilder. 'We begin by assessing the body's musculo-skeletal system to establish where the pain stems from and then treat with manipulative techniques to correct mechanical problems and stimulate the natural healing process.'

Chiropractors are often confused with osteopaths, but in fact specialise in the spine and nervous system, and aim to improve movement, flexibility and communication between the brain and the body by gently adjusting the joints. A study in the *British Medical Journal* found that back pain sufferers having chiropractic treatment improved 29% more than those having conventional physiotherapy.

**Your back will thank you if you work on your core fitness. Turn to Idea 16, *Hard core.***

Try another idea…

Back pain is a mixture of spinal misalignment, muscle spasm, nerve irritation and generalised inflammation. Chiropractors believe that all these factors need to be resolved to allow the back to function properly, and the process may take weeks or months. Stretching and strengthening before you head for the slopes is an important part of the process but, sorry, this isn't a quick fix to squeeze in just before your ski trip.

Finally, physiotherapy is commonly used to treat back pain, and is a good preventative option that may give your back a boost before you hit the slopes. Physiotherapy may involve massage, manipulation and exercises to correct muscle imbalances. However, one recent study published in the *BMJ* found that routine physiotherapy for mild backache seems no more effective than one session of assessment and advice.

**'Happiness is nothing more than good health and a bad memory.'**
An unknown author stumbles on the best back pain remedy.

Defining idea…

A physio will not only aim to get you fixed up in the short term, but will also give you advice to ensure your back pain doesn't return. The vast majority of people who suffer one bout of back pain unfortunately find it returns again later in life. This is where physiotherapy really helps.

25

**How did it go?**

**Q**  **I feel fine on the slopes, it's only afterwards that my back starts to ache. Is there a good stretch I can do to get some relief?**

*A*  *Lie on the ground, back straight, legs out in front of you. Bring your left knee up to 90°, and hold with your right hand. Extend your left arm at 90° to your body. Then slowly drop your left knee towards the right, while keeping both shoulders on the ground. Take it as far as comfortable, hold for 10 seconds, then repeat on the other side. It's also a good idea to do some gentle back stretches before you hit the hill too, to ease your back into the day.*

**Q**  **I think I need better preparation for next season – what exercise do you suggest?**

*A*  *Pilates is your best bet for bad backs. A system of mind-body exercise, originally developed to help ballet dancers strengthen core muscles, it builds strength, body awareness, good posture and good movement, so it's great for getting you more flexible for next year and easing your pain.*

# 7

# The protection racket

**Butt pad, wrist guards, kidney protection – slope style has suddenly gone all Michelin man. But how much protection does body armour really give you?**

Over the last few years, sales of body armour for snowsports have escalated, especially among the more cautious 25-plus age group. But is the Chubba look and the extra outlay worth it?

The first time I swapped my skis for a snowboard, a tender tailbone and a bruised butt soon made me cotton on to the wonders of padding. Only eight years ago it was a few pairs of rolled-up ski socks that cushioned my fall, not a high-tech, no-messing pair of padded shorts.

## TAKE GOOD CARE OF YOURSELF

The market for protective armoury, such as wrist guards, back protectors and padded shorts has exploded. Are we just wimps or can it really help?

Here's an idea for you...

**Learn how to fall safely. If you're on a snowboard falling forwards, try to relax and fall evenly on your protected knees, and forearms. Ball your fists, with your thumb outside, as if you were ready to punch someone, so that your wrists are protected. On skis, falling sideways, try to keep your knees from hitting the snow first as this will tend to twist them. Land instead on your butt.**

Research shows that wearing a helmet substantially reduces your chance of severe injury and can mean the difference between concussion and brain damage.

You might think that helmets are only for people who ride in the trees, or do big tricks. But the first time you catch an edge and the back of your head hits the hard ground, you'll reconsider. I was so desperate to get protection after my first clunk that I forked out for a top-of-the-range helmet when I was still dazed with concussion.

If you're venturing off-piste on rocky or wooded terrain, wearing a helmet can be a genuine life-saver. Most pro freestyle skiers and snowboarders now wear them and they thankfully shed their geeky image long ago. You just have to look at the *über*-cool, best-selling 'bad lieutenant' helmet from Giro to know that helmets have gone beyond safety status to achieve fashion status.

Standards are determined by a battery of tests on helmet models, including testing the strength of a helmet's retention system under simulated hot, cold and wet conditions. Look for the CE mark that shows yours has been through the same.

Next on the list of safety essentials, and one that's invaluable for novice snowboarders, are wrist guards. Some experts argue that wearing skate wrist guards can increase the severity of a fracture by sending the 'shock' up the arm to a larger bone, so try and hunt out a snowboard specific guard. Often built into snowboard gloves, several studies have shown that wrist guards reduce injuries, and their severity, in snowboarders.

**Turn to Idea 15, *Injury-free forever*, for more ways to protect your weak spots.**

*Try another idea…*

As I found out as a beginner boarder, the spine and tailbone are also injury-prone. Many injuries happen on relatively flat slopes with bulletproof snow. Skiers tend to fall more on the side or forwards, and freestyle injuries tend to be the most extreme and long-lasting. All padding can help reduce impact but the best protection is not determined by the thickness of the pad, rather its ability to resist compression. The trick is to spread out the load of impact, so it is less concentrated and results in less damage. Forget the natural padding you may have on your behind; you need padding that's not connected to your central nervous system.

Once you're convinced of the need to save your posterior, invest in some real padding with a hard plastic shell outside and soft padding on the inside.

Look for quality when you are buying body armour. The CE mark shows a product has met high industry standards and undergone rigorous testing.

Most experts agree that padding will certainly reduce 'ouch' moments and may absorb impact, but warn that for many ski injuries it won't provide any protection at all. Twisting and rotation causes many injuries (particularly knee injuries) and body armour will do nothing to help.

Another worry is the 'risk perception' factor. Padded up to the hilt you may feel safer and so take more risks. But still, protection is probably the best method of prevention.

*'The chief danger in life is that you may take too many precautions.'*
ALFRED ADLER

*Defining idea…*

The bottom line? It may pay to pad.

*How did it go?*

**Q**   **What's the best way to fit a helmet?**

**A**   *Your helmet size is determined by the circumference of your head, so grab a tape measure. Next, try on the helmet, lining up the front of the helmet above your eyebrows and holding both straps until the helmet fits well. Check it for gaps between the lining and your head, and make sure the back of the helmet doesn't touch the back of your neck. Finally, give it the wobble test – if it moves when you shake your head, try a smaller size.*

**Q**   **My toe edge is my weaker edge so I always seem to land on my knees. What knee protection can I get?**

**A**   *Knee protection is one of the most important pieces of snowboard protective gear because knees are bony and vulnerable (as well as being complex joints that are painful and expensive to fix). Try wearing knee pads under your snow pants – in-line skate pads are fine. Make sure they are soft and well padded on the inside, and hard plastic to absorb shock and protect on the outside. Good pads will also keep your knees warm and flexible and, because you'll feel more confident about tumbling on your knees, you'll be less likely to stick out your hands to let your wrists break your fall; so you'll protect them too.*

# 8

# Going up

**Grrr, lifts. They save you no end of effort but they also cause you no end of hassle. Lengthy lines, aching legs and how the hell do you get off them?**

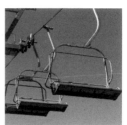

Lifts come in all shapes and sizes — chair-lifts, button lifts, T-bars, rope tows. Sometimes going up can be more daunting than coming down. Don't worry, we're here to make it child's play.

My first dozen attempts on a chair-lift were humiliating, humbling experiences. Just as I'd built up the confidence to link a few turns going downhill, I suddenly took a brutal knock back on the lift to the top. But, had I learnt a few simple tips, it would have been as easy as it's going to be for you.

The first lift you'll have to contend with is the poma, or button, lift that serves the shortest slopes. The golden rule here is not to treat it as a seat. It is not designed to sit on, so keep standing upright with your skis parallel and ankle joints flexed and simply let it pull you. Easy.

**Ready to ride the chair-lift? Take your backpack off first. Sit with it placed in front of you on your lap, hooking your arm through one of the straps to ensure it doesn't fall off. If you don't the straps can easily get caught on the back of the chair and if that happens you'll find yourself riding back down the chair-lift with it too.**

On a snowboard? Unstrap your back foot and skate to the loading area. Point the nose of the board uphill and, as the poma swings around, reach for it with your back hand and put it firmly behind your front thigh, letting it drag you. Stay standing upright, with your back foot on the board wedged against the back binding. Keep your knees soft to absorb any unexpected bumps, keep your weight evenly balanced and don't tense your muscles. If you're dragged across a bumpy section, put a bit more weight on your front foot. You can also ride a poma by holding it with your hands, like a water-ski, but only if the slope is gentle.

Another lift you'll probably ride a lot of, especially in the early days, is the T-bar or drag-lift. Again, they tend to serve the shorter slopes (although the longest T-bar I've ridden was an jelly-leg-inducing 1.6km long!).

On a snowboard, the process is exactly the same as the button; just wedge the 'T' part behind your front thigh and hold on to the post. If you find yourself veering off course, just hold the post with your front hand and pull your trailing shoulder back so that your shoulders form a line with the hill.

On skis it's easiest to ride the T-bar with someone else of a similar height. One side of the 'T' will catch your behind, the other side will catch your lift buddy. As the T-bar comes round, reach for the pole and let the 'T' push you gently forward.

Don't sit down, just let it drag you. Keep your skis parallel and stay relaxed. If you're tense, every bump will make you wobble and you'll quickly get tired.

**The chair-lift is the perfect time to rehydrate and refuel. Turn to Idea 38, *Peak performance*, for sports nutrition know-how.**

*Try another idea…*

## NOW FOR THE BIG ONE …

The most common form of Alpine access and the one you'll be using throughout your snowsports career; the chair-lift. On skis, get your poles out of the way by holding them in one hand and shuffle up to the loading area.

Look behind you as the lift swings round and reach out to grab the seat to avoid the lift slamming into the back of your legs.

If you're on a snowboard, have only your front foot strapped in and point the nose of your board uphill. Let the chair scoop you up and sit down, lifting the nose of your board slightly to clear the loading area.

When you near the top, shuffle forwards on your seat. Skiers can simply stand up and snowplough gently down the run-off. Snowboarders need to twist the board around so that the nose points dead ahead and prepare to place the base of the board flat on the ground. Once it's there, stand up, placing your back foot on the board against your back binding. Keep your knees bent, balance most of your weight on your front foot and simply cruise down the run-off until it feels flat enough to stop.

Finally, if you take a spill, make the most of it. Sharing comedy lift tales is one of the best forms of bonding in the bar later.

*'It's a real primal thing, watching someone get hurt. It's funny and accessible.'*
JOHNNY KNOXVILLE on the consolations of falling off.

*Defining idea…*

33

How did
it go?

**Q** **Terrible. How can I stop panicking and putting my back leg on the ground instead of on my snowboard when I get to the top?**

*A* *The golden rule of staying upright on the run-off on a snowboard is always to keep your back foot placed firmly on the board. If you don't, you'll tumble every time. Try to think of placing that back foot on the board as if it has a magnet on it. Tell yourself it's as immovable as your strapped-in front foot. Wedge your foot up against the back binding so that it feels firm and make sure you have a stomp pad so that your foot has something to grip.*

*Just because your foot isn't in its binding it doesn't mean you're any less stable, so calm down, don't panic and gently cruise down the run-off as you would down any nursery slope.*

**Q** **Ouch, how can I stop my foot getting tired from carrying the whole weight of my snowboard on a chair-lift?**

*A* *Many older lifts don't have footrests on which to balance your board, so you'll need to use your back foot instead. Bring your board parallel to the chair so your toes point forwards and rest the back of your board on the top of your back foot. If it's still throbbing, loosen the straps slightly on your front binding before getting onto the lift.*

# 9

# Park life: snowboard

**Skip the table tops, the jumps and the rails and you miss half of what snowboarding's all about. Everyone has to be a first timer in the park some time.**

The last few years have seen an explosion in freestyle. Whether it's riding rails, hucking in the halfpipe or spinning big airs, freestyle is where it's at. Take a deep breath, you're up.

To the uninitiated and the over-thirties, the terrain park is one of the most intimidating places. Everyone in there seems too cool for school (and that's exactly where most of them should be); it feels as though all eyes are on you and the scope for potential injury – well, it's off the scale.

Luckily, as in most things, perceptions are often wrong. The great thing about snowboarding is that, no matter how good they are now, everyone has been a jelly-legged novice at some point. They know how it feels and this fosters a common feeling of support and encouragement. Feeling warm and gooey yet? Good, because now you know everyone is on your side, dropping in to the park for the first time will be much easier.

Here's an idea for you...

**When entering the park for the first time, take a run through without hitting any of the obstacles, just to check the size of the jumps, the take-offs and landings and the approaches to rails. Everything should be nice and smooth. If not, it may not be the best park to start in because everything will be that much harder and more risky.**

To lay the foundations, practise riding fakie or switch stance (backwards) on the normal slopes to help develop your edge control. Riding fakie is like learning to snowboard all over again. To make it easier, start by simply traversing backwards, as you did when you learnt to get down the hill, falling leaf style, gradually build up to trying turns. All the rules you learned in regular stance apply here too.

Watch other people on a nice easy jump so that you can build a picture of how much speed you need to make it comfortably to the landing. You're looking for a start spot from where you can ride in a straight line without having to put in turns.

Once you've gauged the spot, point your nose at the jump and ride straight, with your weight slightly forward, either on your heel edge or toe edge, never truly a flat base. Bear in mind that if you are on your toe edge you'll find it easier to balance during take-off.

'Keep your weight in the middle of the board and bend your knees to keep low,' advises pro park rider for K2 Pat Meurier. 'Don't lean backwards or forwards and try not to tense up.'

When you take off, bring your legs up underneath you to give better balance through the air. Look for your landing and extend your legs when you hit it, like a car's suspension.

Now add in the fakie stuff you learned earlier by riding forwards across the fall line on your uphill edge. As you approach the jump, lower your body by flexing the knees and look fixedly at the take-off point. Jump, looking in the direction you're going, then turn your back foot around in front of you and let your body spin 180°. Feels good?

**If you're riding rails you'll need to 'detune' your board. Turn to Idea 52, *Love your hardware*, to find out how.**

*Try another idea…*

## LET'S PROGRESS TO RAILS

Ideally your first rail should be a flat bar about half the width of your board, low to the ground with a ramp to ride onto it. Try the 50–50 as your first trick. Start close enough to the rail so that you don't have to turn before you hit it – this will ensure you hit it straight on and flat. Then ride in a straight line towards the ramp, cruise straight onto the rail, along it and straight off it at the other end. Yes, it's that simple.

The secret to pulling it off is to keep your weight even, bend your knees and keep your body and arms low and in the centre of the rail. As you become more comfortable, you can gently slide your board so that it's perpendicular to the rail. If you do this, you must dull your edges – if they're sharp, you're liable to catch one and be unceremoniously dumped off the rail.

*'If we listened to our intellect, we'd never have a love affair. We'd never have a friendship. We'd never go into business, because we'd be too cynical. Well, that's nonsense. You've got to jump off cliffs all the time and build your wings on the way down.'*
ANNIE DILLARD

*Defining idea…*

37

*How did it go?*

**Q** **I didn't understand a word! What park life lingo do I need in my vocabulary?**

A  *Most of the tricks performed in the park came from skateboarding, and you'll find the terminology is pretty similar too. Don't worry about the lingo too much. For now, all you need to know is, if you're spinning frontside, you're turning the same way you would for a heel side turn. If you're spinning backside (or blindside), you're spinning the same way you would for a toe side turn. If you're riding fakie or switch, you're riding backwards as if the tail of the board were the nose.*

**Q** **I got yelled at and I don't know why. Is there any park etiquette I should be aware of?**

A  *Put your awareness on heightened alert when you're in the park, looking around you at all times. Never stand around the landing zones of obstacles and clear the area as quickly as possible. Sounds obvious but we've all done it – easy to do when you're mesmerised watching riders pull big airs. When you're ready to drop in and there's a queue or gathering on the approach: 'Snaking (queue jumping) is frowned upon and can lead to bad karma,' explains experienced park buff and K2 rider Pat Meurier. 'So put your hand up to let others around know your intention to drop in and say "next" if need be.'*

# 10

# Après-ski angels

**Overdosed on après-ski? A bit of pretox and planning for the morning after will get you out on the slopes before lunch.**

For many, the mountain air isn't enough to cut through that thumping headache and fuzzy mind. Here's how to head off a hangover.

Après-ski is as much a part of a snowsports holiday as the piste-bashing itself. Lord knows you've earned it but, if your time on the slopes is as precious as most, the last thing you'll want is to let a hangover gnaw into your snow time the following day.

### PRETOX, NOT DETOX

It goes without saying that the best way to maximise your on-hill performance is to stay on the soft stuff, at least for a few nights of your trip. But if the schnapps, mulled wine or Pinot Noir is too much to resist, forget the drudge of a dreary post-holiday detox and opt for a spot of pretox instead. It's all about damage limitation.

*Here's an idea for you...* **If you're anticipating a series of late nights, pretox by focusing on boosting your nervous system. Try starting your day with a refreshing tea of lemon balm, which is good for the digestion, the nervous system and can help alleviate headaches induced by tiredness.**

Let's start with your liver, the organ that's going to bear the brunt of the après onslaught. You can help it get ready for flushing out toxins, by eating the right foods before you even get to the slopes.

For example, the fat you get from untainted, unprocessed food is the least toxic for your liver. Even if additive-free meals do have fat in them, it's the kind your body knows how to deal with. So eating unprocessed food and plenty of fruit and vegetables in the pre-ski run-up will help. The best pretox heroes include artichoke, broccoli, cabbage, beetroot, onions, apples, grapefruit and figs.

*Defining idea...* *'I have enjoyed great health at a great age because every day since I can remember, I have consumed a bottle of wine except when I have not felt well. Then I have consumed two bottles.'*

A bishop of Seville

Another way to temper the toxic effects of alcohol is to sneak in a sensible snack before you hit the bar. After the pistes, nip back to your chalet or hotel and grab a light pretox snack that combines complex carbohydrate and protein. This can be as simple as an apple and nuts, a chicken sandwich or a crispbread with cottage cheese. All will help slow down the absorption of alcohol.

**All those long days and late nights will take their toll on your immune system, so turn to Idea 12, *The best defence*, for ways to supercharge your defences for the slopes.**

*Try another idea…*

Another sure-fire way to minimise the effects of a hangover is to drink lots of water – not just during and after your après-ski, but in the week before you start it too. Water works because it flushes toxins through your body, improving liver and kidney function and rehydrating your skin.

Build up to significant water consumption gradually over a few days. If you're not used to consuming large amounts, your body won't retain it. Building up to two litres gradually over a week will help your body rehydrate more effectively when it needs to. Drink it straight, in herbal teas, warmed up with a slice of lemon … but drink it, especially just before you go out.

*'Wine … offers a greater range for enjoyment and appreciation than possibly any other purely sensory thing which may be purchased.'*
ERNEST HEMINGWAY

*Defining idea…*

Defining
idea...

*'Wine is at the head of all medicines; where wine is lacking, drugs are necessary.'*
Babylonian *Talmud*: BABA BATHRA.

## HERBAL HELPERS

Now for the no-effort-required options to get you on that black run before noon – herbal heroes.

Milk thistle is one of the best supplements to pop before you drink, as it contains silymarin, which is believed to protect the liver from alcohol damage by stimulating protein synthesis and promoting the regeneration of liver cells. Artichoke extract may aid detoxification too, but there is less research to back up its powers. Other supplements that have given birth to a new generation of remedies to help you exorcise the effects of the demon drink include calcium carbonate and vegetable carbon, which help absorb toxins.

If you're not quick enough to catch your hangover before it starts and awake up to the WBA heavyweight title fight taking place in your head, try the good old 'plink, plink, fizz.' Effervescent vitamin C, painkillers, whatever your tried and tested remedy is.

But remember the very best cure of all that's guaranteed to cut through the fur and filth of a hangover … a blast of fresh mountain air.

**Q   Milk thistle? Pah! I took it with my first drink and had the hangover from hell the next morning. Does this stuff really work?**

*How did it go?*

*A   The research looks good, yes. Milk thistle protects and stimulates the liver but you may have taken it too late. Although 500mg taken even a few hours before a night out will help, it's best to start a week or so before your skiing holiday (and inevitable après-ski) starts.*

**Q   The hangover's one thing, but I tend to get into 'social smoker' mode when I've had a few. How can I cure my inhaled hangover?**

*A   Smoke-filled bars or 'special occasion' cigarettes will be highly toxic to your body. The best foods to combat the effects of smoking or other people's smoke are those rich in antioxidants. Antioxidants play a key role in minimising damage to the cells in our body, and hence slow down the ageing process and help in the fight against disease. Smoking soaks up supplies of the antioxidant vitamin C, so munch on vitamin C-rich foods such as kiwis, papaya, oranges, broccoli and green peppers, the morning after. Selenium and vitamin E may also help to protect the body against the lung damage that smoking and passive smoking cause. Get it from sunflower seeds, Brazil nuts, avocados, almonds and walnuts and dark green leafy vegetables.*

## 11

# Weather any white-out

**Whether you beg, borrow or buy it, there are some criteria your outerwear just has to meet. Don't let the manufacturers blind you with science; gearing up is simpler than they make it sound.**

The key to a happy day on the hill is to make sure you're prepared for whatever the changeable mountain weather throws at you. The secret lies in layers. Here's what you really need to head for the hills.

I cringe to remember my first trip to the slopes. Packed off on a school trip by parents who had never set their feet in skis in their lives, they begged and borrowed what they could for me and 'made do' with the rest. That meant woollen gloves (sopping wet and freezing after two falls), school socks (blister magnets if ever there were) and supermarket sunglasses (not ideal for blizzards).

Never make the mistake of economising on your outerwear – it really will make or break your whole day in the snow. These days, of course, we're spoilt for choice. Fabric technology is space age and we've learnt a thing or two about what works in the white stuff.

**Here's an idea for you...** **Don't forget your feet. Ideally you should wear the socks you'll wear on the mountain when you go shopping for boots. Too thick and you'll lose responsiveness; too thin and you'll get cold feet. Ski or snowboard specific socks may seem like a gimmick, but they're really not, and the anatomic padding is worth the expense.**

## ONE DARNED THING ON TOP OF ANOTHER

The key to a toasty trip is to think in layers. Ideally, you need three layers that include warmth, wicking (or moisture management) and waterproofing. As the temperature changes, so can your number of layers.

Most important is the outer layer, the shell that protects against wind and snow. Your jacket is probably the piece of clothing you'll fork out the most for, possibly more for fashion reasons than anything else. It is after all, what sets your on-piste identity. And thankfully, fashion no longer has to sacrifice function – fabrics are more technical and better than ever.

The basic jacket requirements are to be waterproof and windproof. Generally clothing can be called waterproof when it can bear a water column of 120 to 150 cm, which means that when a hollow tube is filled with water up to that height, none of it gets through the fabric. The best jackets can withstand a water column of more than 10m. If a jacket can withstand 10m of water, it's also likely to be windproof, which can make a big difference on a blustery day. Seams are also important for keeping out the wet stuff. The best come with taped seams and covered zippers.

The other key requirement you want in a jacket is breathability. You lose more than half a litre of fluid through your skin each day when you're just sitting still, so imagine how much you lose on the hill. You don't want this to accumulate inside your jacket, so look for fabric that 'breathes'. If you're skiing in the spring, consider a light-weight shell, which is moisture repellent and protects from wind, but doesn't keep you dry in a blizzard, or warm in −20°C winds.

**Stay at the cutting edge of cool by choosing the gear of the future. Turn to Idea 51, *Cutting edges*.**

*Try another idea...*

Your snow pants make up the outer layer on your legs and should meet the same criteria. They should also have an elasticated 'snow skirt' at the bottom of each leg to keep out powder. If you're a boarder, it's also a good idea to get pants with reinforced backside and knee sections – you'll be spending a lot of time on both! Don't even think of wearing jeans. The snow will melt, soak into the fabric and freeze. If you want the denim look, hunt out the new waterproof denim-look fabrics that are now being used for snow pants.

A fleece makes the perfect middle layer because it has thermal properties that enable the body to breathe by allowing sweat to evaporate. It can be left in the hotel or stashed in your backpack on warmer days.

Finally, a good base layer begins with thermal pants and top that keeps you warm and dry by transferring, or wicking, moisture away from the body to the next layer.

Remember to accessorise right too: a hat or helmet and UV protective goggles (sunnies are fine on a blue sky day, but useless when descending at speed in the cold or snow). Oh, and a good pair of waterproof, padded gloves are essential too – wool, I can testify, doesn't work well with snow.

*'The sport of skiing consists of wearing $3000-worth of clothes and equipment and driving two hundred miles in the snow in order to stand around at a bar and get drunk.'*

P.J. O'ROURKE, *Modern Manners*

*Defining idea...*

*How did it go?*

**Q  My mate warned me to wear synthetics rather than natural fabrics because they breathe better – is this true?**

A  *It used to be, but it's not any more. Generally natural fabrics can't wick moisture away from the body, but with the development of merino wool from New Zealand things have changed. Merino wicks just as well as the high-tech synthetics and feels super-soft (not itchy), so is a good choice for base layers.*

**Q  I've got dark lenses on my goggles and find it hard to see on dull days. Can I change them?**

A  *Yes, lenses come in a whole rainbow of colours for different light conditions. Your black, polarised lenses reduce glare without distorting colours and are great for bright sunny conditions. Green or silver lenses are also good in these conditions and enhance contrast.*

   *On darker days, you'll be better off with yellow, orange or gold lenses, which filter out blue light and bring out shadows, making them good for most conditions and especially in low light. Purple and pinkish lenses also help bring out the shadows and contours of the slopes, so are good for darker days.*

## 12

# The best defence

**It's cold, it's wet and you'll be out in it every day, but the last thing you want is to fall sick on your precious week in the snow. So boost your immune system now and make sure your defences are tip-top in time.**

First you've got to survive the germ-rife plane cabin; next, cope with the onslaught of sub-zero temperatures; and finally your body has to protect itself from late nights, early mornings and hangovers. You'd better start winter-proofing your body now!

Your immune system is a complex network of organs that includes the spleen, bone marrow, tonsils, adenoids (the tissue at the back of your throat) and the lymphatic system. It's going to come in for a bit of a bashing during the chilly ski season, but there are plenty of ways you can help it in its battle against infection.

Here's an
idea for
you...

**Thinking happy thoughts boosts the immune system, stressful thoughts can lower levels of immune antibodies. Whenever you feel stressed, close your eyes, take five deep, slow breaths and recall a happy memory. Stay focused on it for five minutes and open your eyes again.**

## SMART EATING

The simplest and most effective change you can make to fire up those defences is to your diet. The bad news is, that means keeping all those yummy foods containing sugar and saturated fat to a minimum in the run-up to your ski trip. Not only do they suppress your immune system but they also put more stress on your liver, which, let's face it, is probably going to be working overtime once you hit holiday mode.

The best foods for boosting your immune system are those containing high levels of anti-oxidant vitamins A, C, E and the minerals zinc and selenium. Good choices are green tea, Brazil nuts, almonds, sunflower seeds, sweet potato, green leafy vegetables; fruit such as grapes, watermelon, guava, grapefruit and especially those rich in lycopene like tomatoes.

Garlic is also a good weapon to have in your armoury, as it is known to fight bacterial, fungal and viral infections. It also reduces inflammation and benefits the heart and circulatory system, thanks to its sulphur compounds, which support the action of killer cells – cells designed to fight off foreign bodies.

Finally, probiotics, the 'friendly' bacteria found in live yoghurt and other cultured or fermented foods, are seen as the latest essential immune-pumping allies. Probiotics, either in food or supplement form, have been shown to improve the body's resistance to bacterial and viral infections.

**Laid up sick? You can still improve your skiing or snowboarding by using the time to practise visualisation – see Idea 35, *Winning the mind game.***

*Try another idea...*

## POP SOME OF THESE

It will probably pay to pop a few of the right supplements in the run-up to winter too, as late nights and drinking will take their toll and increase your susceptibility to viruses and infections.

Personally, I swear by the cold-busting duo vitamin C and zinc when I'm feeling under the weather, and the research seems to back me up, with some studies showing they help prevent colds and flu and reduce their severity if you do succumb.

Research into vitamin E also shows that it may reduce your susceptibility to infections – a good idea when you're going to be spending a lot more time in hot, crowded bars.

**'A bad cold wouldn't be so annoying if it weren't for the advice of our friends.'**
KIN HUBBARD

*Defining idea...*

The herb echinacea is also a staple in the army of defence boosters, although the scientific community is divided over whether it really works. There are as many studies revealing its positive effects as those saying it doesn't work, but it is believed to work by increasing the number of white blood cells in the body that fight off germs. It may also raise the production of interferon, a protein that prevents the virus from reproducing in cells, killing off the infection. Take it for no more than six to eight weeks at a time.

## RAISE YOUR EXERCISE LEVEL

Regular, moderate exercise has also been shown to improve immunity too. So, as well as getting your body fit for the onslaught of intense exercise in the mountains, you'll also have better defences if you up your exercise about six weeks before you go.

Exercise increases the number of natural killer (NK) cells in your body. These lymphocytes in the bloodstream and the mucosal layer of the nose and airways travel around your body scavenging foreign invaders such as bacteria and viruses. When you exercise, NK levels rise and stay elevated for about 36 hours.

**Q**    **I felt fine physically but was swamped with work before I left – as soon as I relaxed on day one of my holiday I fell sick. Why?**

*How did it go?*

*A*    *This is a classic symptom of work-focused societies, recently dubbed 'leisure sickness' by the experts. If you have loads of last minute work deadlines to cope with before you get to take off to the slopes, take a course of B-Complex vitamins to combat the symptoms of stress and support immune function.*

**Q**    **I think I caught a cold on the flight out. I feel awful – should I hit the hill or will that just make it worse?**

*A*    *Don't struggle out to the snow if you feel truly dreadful, as this will increase your risk of dehydration and could make you worse. Your body needs to save its energy for fighting the infection. If you don't have a temperature and are desperate not to waste a single day, do the 'neck check'. If your symptoms are above the neck (stuffy nose, watery eyes, sniffles) try riding but take it easier than normal. If they're below the neck (chills, coughing, aches and nausea), put your feet up in the chalet and dream of how you'll ride tomorrow.*

# 13
# Skin saviours

**The sun is stronger, the winds are harsher and the 'hat hair' hidden for most of the day does you no favours when you hit the bar. If you want to stay gorgeous and healthy below zero, you've gotta work at it.**

Biting winds, snow glare and central heating can wreak havoc with your skin.
If you aren't aware already (and apparently dozens of weathered ski instructors aren't), the laws of skin care change with the seasons. Here's what really works in your winter armoury.

You change your clothes but do you change your skin care? What works for your skin during the warm (well, warmish) months of summer, won't necessarily work when you head to the ski slopes, start exercising outdoors or simply sit in centrally heated buildings come winter.

'During the winter, skin is exposed to dry, indoor heat with less humidity,' explains Dr Chérie M. Ditre, a dermatologist at University of Pennsylvania. 'Add to that the

*Here's an idea for you...* **The combined drying effects of the sun, wind and central heating can leave your skin gasping for moisture. Combat the dry air of your hotel room or chalet by filling a sink full of hot water before you go to sleep. It will add moisture to the air and help your skin feel more comfortable.**

heavy, bulky clothes and the skin begins to generate less of its own natural moisturisers, especially as we age, which can lead to flakiness and itching.'

In humid conditions, your skin can replenish itself by soaking up moisture from the air but when the humidity drops, your skin loses another opportunity to moisturise itself. Couple that with the low humidity of indoor heating, as well as hot showers and baths, and your skin is bound to become dry and irritated.

The best way to keep the skin healthy is to replenish its moisture (yep, you too, boys). Avoid long, hot baths that can dry the skin and instead take tepid showers, using a moisturising body wash and apply a moisturiser within three minutes of stepping out of the shower to trap water in the upper layers of the skin.

Boring I know, but now, more than any other time of year, you also need to drink lots of water. Aim to rehydrate yourself before you start feeling thirsty, especially if you're out riding on the hill. A humidifier can also counteract dry heat at home, but a bath full of warm water can work just as well if you're in a hot hotel or chalet.

If you find your normal body moisturiser isn't getting rid of dryness, don't just slap on more. Instead, go for a richer product such as something containing cocoa butter or shea butter.

Regular exfoliation can also help boost the efficacy of your moisturiser.

'If your skin becomes drier in winter, look for a milder soap that is fragrance-free or one that contains moisturising ingredients, like oils and vitamins, which can be beneficial for your skin all year round,' suggests Ditre.

Wash your face with lukewarm water and a mild facial cleanser. If you have oily skin, don't assume that you need a moisturiser. Wait 20 minutes after washing and if your face feels tight, use a moisturiser only where you feel dry.

'Retinoids can be used to decrease acne and oiliness, reduce the appearance of fine lines, wrinkles and age spots, and help prevent the signs of ageing,' adds Ditre. 'But products containing retinoids may be drying and increase the chance of skin flaking and redness, so it's important to talk with a dermatologist or skin care expert about how to offset the effects of winter.'

Even if you're a guy who doesn't believe you need to slather yourself in products to look good, the one thing you will certainly need is a good sunscreen. Snow can reflect more than 80% of the sun's damaging ultraviolet radiation, so it's important to always wear a broad-spectrum sunscreen with an SPF of 15 or higher, especially on exposed body parts such as the face, hands, lips and tops of the ears. Try and ensure you stop regularly to top up your sun cream. Time flies when the

**Try another idea...**

**Your clothes and equipment can protect your skin too. Turn to Idea 51, *Cutting edges*, to find out about the cutting edge of snowsports.**

**Defining idea...**

*'Some people, no matter how old they get, never lose their beauty – they merely move it from their faces into their hearts.'*

MARTIN BUXBAUM

57

slopes are working, but don't let that 'one more run' temptation leave you with a bad sunburn.

How did it go?

**Q** **I religiously exfoliate in winter to keep skin smooth, but will it make my skin more sensitive to the elements?**

A *Yes. Be especially careful when using alpha-hydroxy acid products. They exfoliate the top layer of the skin leaving the new layer of skin unprotected to the elements, including the sun and bitter winds.*

**Q** **I'm all sorted on the skin protection front, it's my straw-like hat hair I'm worried about. Any advice?**

A *The sun and temperature extremes will suck the moisture from your locks in no time so prepare your hair by putting in a bit of preparation before your holiday. Use an intensive conditioning treatment a few weeks before you go to help build up the moisture content of your hair and keep it glossy. To really get the most out of a treatment, wrap your hair in cling-film after applying the conditioner and leave it for a few minutes.*

*Once you're out there, I'm afraid 'hat hair' really is the best option as it will protect your tresses from getting frazzled by the sun.*

# 14

# Pre-ski prep

**We've all been there … you wake up on day two of your ski holiday and your body refuses to move. Avoid the agony by working on your ski fitness before you go.**

How many millions of snow sports devotees spend an entire year living the life of a couch potato then suddenly exercise to the max for one full week? Neglect your fitness in the off-season and, ouch, you'll pay for it come winter.

If you're anything like most of my ski and snowboard buddies, you'll spend a frantic week before you depart on your ski trip madly training in the gym to counteract the effects of a particularly sedentary festive season. Deep down we all know it – seven days of treadmill devotion and a few token squat thrusts aren't going to supercharge you on the slopes.

Here's an idea for you...

**If you only do one ski-specific exercise in the run-up to your trip, make it 'the chair'. With your ankles, knees and hips at 90° keep your back straight against the wall and pretend you are sitting on a chair. Keep your lower back in a strong straight position by sucking in the stomach. Hold for as long as possible and time yourself. Start with 10 seconds and aim to build up to two to five minutes. Aim to beat your last time every week.**

## FITNESS TAKES TIME; SO THIS YEAR, WHY NOT START EARLY?

Ideally you need to get started at least six weeks before you hit the slopes and aim to exercise three or four times a week for 45 minutes to an hour.

Aerobic cardiovascular exercise that pumps the heart and lungs (yes, that means getting out of breath) is vital to boost your on-hill fitness. Running, cycling and swimming are all great choices. In the gym, the rowing machine and cross-trainer are the best pieces of kit to use to get in good ski shape. Rollerblading is also good because you'll be using the same motions and muscles as you would on snow, so that you train appropriate muscles and you'll be helping your balance at the same time.

If you're generally fit and healthy, you ideally need to be training at an intensity of 70% of your maximum heart rate to reap the benefits. To get a rough calculation of yours, take 220 and subtract your age. For example, if you are 40, your maximum heart rate would be about 180 beats per minute (bpm), and your training heart rate would be 126 bpm.

Snowsports mean a lot of stop-start exercising. That means interval training is an excellent way to get ski fit. To interval train, push yourself to work out at a high intensity for a short period, then slow right down. For example, you could run at full pelt for 30 seconds, then slow to a gentle jog for a minute, before running flat out again for another 30 seconds and then slowing, and so on. Interval training works with any kind of aerobic exercise and will build your endurance and help you concentrate for longer on the hill.

**Feeling honed and toned? Go one better and target those deep core muscles that boost your on-slope balance in Idea 16, *Hard core*.**

*Try another idea...*

## RIGHT, NOW IT'S TIME TO STRENGTHEN YOUR SKIING AND SNOWBOARDING MUSCLES

Aim to do strength-training exercises two to three times a week. If you are a member of a gym, ask your gym instructor to provide you with a weights programme that will help with your skiing fitness. If you're not a gym bunny, there are still plenty of exercises you can do at home. Try starting with these:

- Crunches – Do a slow sit up, focusing on using your abdominal muscles and raising slowly. Do not pull on your neck. Start with three sets of 15.
- Squat – With legs hip-width apart, toes pointing out and knees aligned over them, slowly begin to 'sit' down as if beginning to sink into a chair. Pretend you're holding ski poles and hold for 30 seconds. Repeat 10 times.
- Striding lunge – Keeping your back straight, stride forwards and lower your rear knee down so that it is just off the ground. Hold, then stride forward with the other leg. Do three sets of 10–20.
- Calf raises – Standing up, raise up slowly onto tiptoes, hold for two seconds and lower slowly. Start with three sets of 10.

*'You can't get up to the slopes and expect your body to do something that it can't even do on dry land.'*
– LINDA CROCKETT
of the Professional Ski Instructors
of America.

*Defining idea...*

61

How did it go?

**Q** **My schedule is so busy that I just can't be bothered with the gym at the end of the day. How can I stay motivated?**

*A* *Try setting yourself a goal and recording your progress. Research shows that people who set measurable, time-framed goals and record their progress, are more likely to stick to it and succeed than those who just try to 'do their best'. So, get a workout diary and set yourself small goals, such as running 5km in less than 30 minutes within two weeks. Log details of each workout, noting small improvements, such as lifting more weights, doing more repetitions and running or cycling further*

**Q** **I'm going snowboarding for the first time this year and I've heard it can be tough on your arms. Are there any specific exercises that will help ease the pain?**

*A* *Yes, novice snowboarders spent at least half their time pushing up off their arms to stand up again after a fall or a rest, and most beginners know that dead arm feeling at the end of the day. It's your triceps that come in for the biggest licking, so prepare by doing tricep dips every other day. Sit at the edge of a chair or bench with your hands clasped over the edge. Using your arms to support you, gently shuffle your feet forward and lower your body down towards the floor (don't touch it though), keeping your hands on the chair and your elbows behind you, bent at 90°. Lower and raise 15 times, rest, and do the same again.*

# 15

# Injury-free forever

**Don't let an injury ruin your next ski trip. Strengthen your weak spots and stay injury-free.**

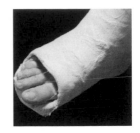

To make sure you get the most out of the holiday you need to be in tip-top condition when you hit the slopes. Here's what it takes to ski all day and have enough energy left to party all night.

Despite what you might think (how hard can gliding downhill and riding a lift uphill be?), snowsports are demanding. If you haven't prepared your body, you'll tire faster, ache earlier and stand a much greater chance of getting injured.

Even gentle coasting makes huge demands on your body. Snow is rarely consistent and you'll be amazed at how much effort your muscles have to summon to cope with ever-changing terrain and snow types.

## SHAPING UP BEFORE YOU START

The muscles we work on the ski hill are often the very ones that we let lie dormant in the off-season. If you don't wake them up ahead of time, your body will have a

Here's an idea for you...

**Working on your balance and co-ordination will help you stay on your feet and recover from a potential wipe-out at speed. If you have access to a wobble board in a gym, use that to practise balancing; otherwise, stand on one leg and with the other leg try and draw numbers 1–10 in the air with your foot.**

rude awakening you'll know all about. Most snowsports injuries happen in the first few days of skiing and at the end of the day when you're tired. But, if you put in some prehab, you can wake up your body in time.

First off, you're going to need a good level of aerobic fitness so that you can last longer and are less likely to pull an injury through fatigue.

To enhance your endurance, you're looking for any regular exercise that raises your heart-beat for prolonged periods. Jogging, power walking, swimming and cycling are all good choices, but any way you can improve your cardiovascular system will help to improve your skiing stamina. If you're not a gym bunny, even going for a brisk walk every day will give you a decent cardiovascular workout. Hill running, stair climbing and inline skating are even better options because they use similar muscles to skiing.

'Plyometric exercises', such as jumping from standing, bounding or making other explosive movements, will also help fine-tune your muscles for snowsports' stop-start nature.

You can also prepare your snowsports-specific muscles with strength-training or lifting weights. Ask the instructor at your gym for a series of strength training exercises that isolate specific leg muscles used in skiing or snowboarding. For example, if you ski a lot, your legs are likely to be stronger on the outside than on the inside, but it's important to get the inside of the leg strong so the kneecap can be held centred and won't be vulnerable to injury. Simple squats, crouching down with your back straight and knees forming a right angle, or lunges are all good options.

Skip the weights machines and choose free weights instead. When you're wedged against a machine while lifting, muscle groups are isolated so that you only train one group. Free weights force you to use balance and a greater range of motion that is more akin to skiing and boarding.

**A strong core is vital for avoiding injury so turn to Idea 16, *Hard core*, and get honing.**

*Try another idea…*

Don't forget that muscles groups work in pairs, so don't just train what you see when you look in the mirror. So, once you've worked your all-important quads and abdominals, remember to also train your opposing muscles, your lower back and hamstrings, to balance out.

Don't neglect your upper body, either. If you're a boarder this is especially important so that you don't injure yourself with all that pushing off the snow you'll be doing to stand up. Press-ups are good preparation.

## THE F WORD – FLEXIBILITY

This is possibly the most important factor in preventing injuries. If you have good range of movement in your joints your body will be better able to adjust to any sudden changes in direction and also help prevent an injury when you fall.

Stretch all of your muscle groups for at least 30 seconds after every workout. Pay special attention to the tendons and ligaments surrounding your joints – they'll need to be flexible, but strong to prevent injury.

*'Any workout which does not involve a certain minimum of danger or responsibility does not improve the body – it just wears it out.'*

NORMAN MAILER

*Defining idea…*

**How did it go?**

**Q**   **I've come back from my ski holiday with aching muscles and blue bruises – anything I can do to speed up my recovery?**

*A*   *Plenty! Treat yourself to a massage to minimise any swelling of the muscles, and to relax sore muscles. Rubbing arnica into bruises can help too. If your gym has a sauna, make the most of it – sweating helps rid the body of toxins and increases circulation to fight aches and pains and speed up the healing process.*

*If you're prone to aches and injury, rub your calves and quads with some oil before you ski. It will bring blood to the area and start to loosen things up.*

**Q**   **I've only got six weeks until I hit the slopes – is it too late to start an injury prevention programme?**

*A*   *No. The earlier you start, the better but it's never too late. Even if you haven't been conscientious about training throughout the off-season, it's the six weeks before the season that are the most important in strength-training and anaerobic conditioning. If you put in the effort now, your body will thank you for it and aching legs and niggling injuries may become a thing of the past.*

*It's important to stretch every day and incorporate some form of aerobic training three or four times per week for at least 30 minutes. Do your anaerobic work (interval training) and weights on at least two days per week – and don't forget to rest! At least one rest day a week is crucial.*

# 16

# Hard core

**It's not just about being able to 'bend ze knees'; the secret to performing on the slopes is balance. Breathe in, it's time to tone that tum and get to the core of ski fitness.**

*'Core stability' has been a buzz phrase in fitness for the last few years and has transformed training.*

Enough of the half-hearted sit-ups and the lazy lunges. If you want to build real strength you need to engage your core muscles.

Your core muscles run from your hips through your pelvis and torso to your shoulder girdle. They help to provide a stable platform for your other muscles to work from, so boosting your balance, and protecting your entire back and pelvis from injury.

Once you've created strong core muscles, you'll really notice the difference on the slopes. All of them help to stabilise the spine while the rest of the body gets in on the action. But you need to train these stabilising muscles in the way that they are going to be used on the slopes. So endless abdominal crunches or sit-ups will only help you so far.

**Make sure you select the right size Swiss ball. Try it out – when you sit on the ball, your knees should be bent to 90° with your feet flat on the floor. Your hips should be bent to almost 90° but should be resting at the same height or slightly higher than your knees.**
**Take care when choosing a stretch band too. Longer is always better as you can wind it up or shorten it. Start with a lighter resistance than you think you need, because a stretch band provides continuous resistance.**

## TRY THESE FUNCTIONAL SNOWSPORTS-SPECIFIC EXERCISES

The core muscle groups that are most important for skiing and snowboarding are the transverse abdominis, the internal and external obliques, the rectus abdominis, the erector spinae and the pelvic floor muscles.

There are several core muscle groups that are important for skiing and snowboarding. The major one is the transverse abdominis, the deepest muscle of the abdominal wall. You'll find it just below your belly button wrapping around your entire body. It stabilises your pelvis and spine when you move and, on the slopes, it helps hold your body upright and balanced.

Strengthen this core stabiliser by doing a 'bridge' or a 'plank'. Starting from lying face down on the floor, place your elbows directly below your body and lift off the ground from your knees, keeping the body in a straight line and the abdominal muscles contracted. Hold for 10 seconds. As you get stronger, try the same exercise but lifting up from your toes. Your obliques, on your sides, are also vital core muscles for riding. These are what allow you to rotate your trunk and bend the body to the side. In snowboarding especially, you often rotate your body and legs to opposite sides to turn, so honing these babies is all-important.

Work the obliques by sitting on the floor with your knees bent and upper body lowered to a 45° angle. Hold a medicine ball in your hands and rotate your upper body from side to side. As well as giving your obliques a good workout, this exercise will also get your transverse abdominis working as it stabilises your lower body, just as it would going down the ski hill.

If you're prone to an aching back when you're on the hill, work on your erector spinae muscles ahead of time. These run up the spine on both sides and are constantly engaged when you ride because you are leaning forward most of the time.

A good back extension exercise that also uses your other core muscles is to lie face down over a stability ball. Position the ball under your hips and pelvis and lean your upper body over the other side. With feet on

**Put in the prep? Don't let it go to waste when you hit the hill. Turn to Idea 17, *Body shock*, for the smartest ways to warm up.**

*Try another idea...*

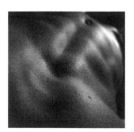

'*We mimic movements in our sport to be better at it. The only limitation until now was that we couldn't duplicate the unbalanced surface that athletes experience when participating in their sport.*'
Reebok gets excited about its ultimate core fitness gadget, the Core Board.

*Defining idea...*

the floor, your elbows out to the side and hands placed behind your head, slowly raise your head and back until your body is in a straight line. Then slowly lower. Always remember to do some light dynamic warm-up exercises before you start (such as long leg swings, walking while raising your knees high and gentle running) and cool down and stretch out your core muscles afterwards.

How did it go?

**Q    I can't remember a long list of exercises and don't really have time anyway. Is there a simple all-round core exercise I can easily remember to tag on the end of my usual workout?**

A    *Invest in a Swiss ball and simply use it for sitting on whenever you can. That way you'll start to strengthen your core muscles without even realising it. If you only learn one 'exercise', a good all round core conditioner that will improve balance and stability on the slopes, is kneeling on your hands and knees on the stability ball. This creates instability in the body and encourages the core muscles to work very hard to keep you from falling off the ball. It's tricky to begin with, but you'll quickly build up to balancing for minutes at a time.*

**Q    My balance is terrible but I don't want to have to buy any of those core-exercising gadgets to improve it. Is there a simple, gimmick-free exercise I can do?**

A    *Balance is vital to your performance on the hill and you don't have to spend a fortune to develop it. Try this easy exercise. Place a tennis ball under the ball of each foot and try to balance, not allowing any other part of your foot to touch the ground. Hold onto a wall until you are balanced then build up to performing small squats on the tennis balls while keeping your balance.*

# 17
# Body shock

**Does your pre-ski routine mean stepping out from hot chocolate and a toasty chalet straight into minus temperatures and a rigorous black run? Give your body a break and warm up before getting down.**

What is your pre-slope warm-up? A leisurely stroll to the cable-car? A hamstring stretch on the gondola? A mug of coffee? If it's any of these it's time to wise up, because research suggests we've got warm-ups all wrong.

OK, so pulling stretches in the lift queues looks a little geeky, and executing star jumps in the gondola won't make you popular, but a bit of preparation before you hit the slopes could transform an average day into a perfect day.

Warming up to raise your core body temperature is crucial to prepare your body for a day on the slopes. Most people (even some of the pros) don't do anything, but you'll ski or ride better if you take 10 minutes to prepare.

Here's an idea for you… **Try yoga's sun salutation to start your day. Inhale as you extend and exhale as you fold. Begin standing feet hip width apart, hands in prayer position. Raise your arms overhead and gently arch your back. Bend forward and bring your hands to rest beside your feet. Inhale and step the right leg back. Exhale and step the left leg back into a 'plank' position. Lower yourself as if coming down from a push-up. Only your hands and feet should touch the floor. Stretch forward and up, bending at the waist. Lift your legs up so that only the tops of your feet and your hands touch the floor. Lift from the hips and push back and up into 'downward dog' pose. Step the right foot forward. Bring the left foot forward and step into head-to-knee position. Rise slowly while keeping arms extended. End standing with hands in prayer position.**

## WARM-UP OR STRETCH?

But, before you reach for your ankles and launch into a series of classic stretches, take note: the jury is out on whether pre-ski stretches will do you any good at all. Static stretches, particularly if done outside before you head for the slopes, are now thought to be a bad idea. Muscles don't stretch well in the cold and research from Australia actually suggests you can increase the risk of injury with pre-exercise stretches. In the study, 2,600 Army recruits were monitored for a year. Half were given stretches to perform before exercise sessions and the other half did not stretch at all over a 12-week period. There were no differences in injury rates between the two groups throughout the course of training, though the overall injury rates were high (20% in 12 weeks). As a result the authors advised the Army to cease pre-exercise stretching.

So why does stretching have such little effect? There's actually very little resemblance between that act of stretching out a muscle and the contractions that muscles undergo during a typical workout. When skiing or snowboarding, you rely on neurological messages to the brain that tell your muscles what to do. What gets these neuromuscular messages moving more quickly is raising your core body temperature, and stretching has no effect on that at all so won't reduce your risk of injury.

A warm-up and pre-exercise stretching are not the same thing. Stretching involves putting muscles in extended positions and holding them there. Warming up involves using muscles in the way you plan to use them, but at a lower intensity, so you increase blood flow in the muscles and get them used to contracting in the way they'll need to for the exercise.

Instead of stretching, look for ways to raise your core temperature to get your lungs and heart working and to get fluid in your joints. Go for big aerobic movements like star jumps, squats and lunging from side to side. But good skiing and boarding are as much in the mind as down to physical skill, which is why a discipline like yoga makes for the ideal pre-slope warm-up.

If you're really serious about your warm-ups, get yourself some lessons in Kum Nye, an ancient Tibetan exercise system that is possibly the perfect pre-ski preparation.

**Banish the burning thighs by putting in the exercise prep before you go. Idea 14, *Pre-ski prep*, shows you how.**

*Try another idea…*

**'I have to exercise in the morning before my brain figures out what I'm doing.'**
MARSHA DOBLE

*Defining idea…*

Originally it was designed to prepare warriors for war in mind, body and spirit. Kum Nye is designed for strength, endurance, flexibility and focus, so is ideal for pre-ski training. But the best thing about Kum Nye is that it consists of just eight simple, dynamic and hellishly hard-to-hold postures, and can be done in its entirety in just 20 minutes, working the heart and all the muscle groups in the process but especially the thighs and buttocks, all-important muscles for skiing and boarding.

*How did it go?*

**Q**  **If I'm wasting my time stretching before I ride, what about afterwards?**

**A**  *No, stretching after your ski day is a different kettle of fish, and a very wise idea if you don't want to feel stiff the next day. A large number of studies carried out in the medical field have shown that stretching stimulates the passage of amino acids into muscle cells, accelerates protein synthesis inside the cells, and slows protein degradation. In English, that means post-workout stretching should help muscle cells repair themselves.*

**Q**  **Surely stretching should help reduce my chances of getting injured, though?**

**A**  *Er, sorry, not if you're pulling static stretches, no. According to the boffins, you have the same risk of getting injured whether you stretch before exercise or not. Why? Most injuries, such as muscle pulls and tears, happen as a result of muscle failure or weakness, not a lack of flexibility. Instead, concentrate on strengthening muscles before you hit the slopes and on warming up the whole body by doing a couple of gentle green or blue runs before you hit the tough stuff.*

# 18

# Stress-free injuries

**Injury is probably the last thing on your mind when you're ripping up the slopes, but a little preparation can save you a lot of heartache.**

If you're unfortunate enough to come a cropper on the ski hill this season, put in the preparation now and you'll have a much easier ride when it comes to injury dilemmas.

The snowsports injury – it's a rite of passage for any hard core snow junkie. My first (and, touch wood, only) snowboarding injury happened very early on in my riding days. And to be honest, I'm glad it happened then, because the blood wagon, heli ride and short spell in hospital taught me a lot about being prepared.

## BE WELL COVERED

The Holy Grail of pre-holiday prep is getting good insurance. Don't skimp on it. Before you buy a policy, check it covers you for everything, including off-piste and snowparks. Medical, air ambulance cover and personal liability should be at least £2 million.

Here's an idea for you…

**Always ski or snowboard with a credit card on you. I learnt from bitter experience that if you injure yourself, you and your ski buddy could be ambulanced a long way from your resort and may have to stay there for a few nights. Nurses' hospitality only gets you so far, no matter how much charm you turn on.**

If you're in Europe, an E111 entitles you to reciprocal state medical cover and negates any excesses on your insurance, but it won't cover repatriation, personal liability, private medical costs or physiotherapy, so separate insurance is essential, especially in Switzerland, and of course in North America (try being told your treatment is about to cost you thousands of dollars when you're drifting in and out of consciousness and you'll see why insurance is so vital).

If you do take a tumble, get someone to cross their skis higher up the mountain to warn others, and alert ski patrol. Always carry proof of insurance on you, tell your friends where it is and make sure someone knows to show it to ski patrol immediately. This should ease your passage off the mountain and you won't have to pay up front.

You and your party should know in advance who to call for 24-hour assistance and should ring as soon as possible. It's also a good idea to carry a credit card and to leave copies of your insurance with a friend at home, just in case.

If the accident is someone else's fault, you'll benefit from independent witness statements (not just from your mates, who may be perceived as biased) so ensure someone in your group carries a pen and paper. If you injure someone else, never admit liability. Exchange details by all means but admitting liability could prejudice your defence.

## SHOULD I STAY OR SHOULD I GO?

But the biggest injury dilemma comes after the initial drama when you're weighing up your treatment options. Should you fly home to get fixed where you know the language, will get continuity of treatment and may feel more comfortable, or should you stay and get patched up by local medics used to dealing with ski injuries?

Some injuries travel better than others, so it depends on what you've done. After basic treatment, injuries to the upper limbs, like sprains and dislocations, travel fine. 'Provided you haven't damaged nerves or blood vessels, you should be safe to travel,' says ski injury specialist Dr David Hughes. 'Even minor fractures to the fingers, thumb or wrist, once stabilised, shouldn't stop you from travelling home for treatment.'

But if your fracture is serious or you've damaged nerves or blood vessels, you'll need emergency treatment before you can fly. 'Always ask questions,' advises Hughes. 'You need to understand the rationale for decisions about timing and where you get treatment. Satisfy yourself that the person treating you has experience with your condition.'

Lower limb injuries are more awkward. If your injury causes your knee or lower leg to swell, delay flying home if the flight is longer than two hours. 'Any swelling severe enough to cause a limp will increase your risk of deep vein thrombosis (DVT), even without flying,' warns Hughes. 'Combining the two can be a recipe for disaster.'

*Try another idea...*

**Why get hurt in the first place? Turn to Idea 15, *Injury-free forever*, to learn how to injury-proof your body.**

*Defining idea...*

**'Skiing is the only sport where you spend an arm and a leg to break an arm and a leg.'**
Author unknown

79

**How did it go?**

**Q** **I've been given the all clear to fly home after taking a bad knock. Any advice?**

**A** *If the medics give you the all clear to travel, rest, ice and elevate your injury and apply a compression bandage. Don't stand around or drink alcohol (tempting if you're trying to block out the pain) because this will exacerbate the swelling. Take a low dose (100mg) of aspirin prior to the flight to thin your blood and do in-flight exercises every half hour. Then seek medical advice as soon as you arrive home.*

**Q** **I can't understand a word that the resort medics are telling me and I don't have faith in them – what shall I do?**

**A** *If in doubt, contact your own GP or a reliable sports physician at home. If you don't have confidence in the medics in resort, or you are in a remote area but can't yet fly home, ask to be transferred to a major referral centre instead. Always tell your insurer too and ask if they can help out.*

# 19

# Have a knees up

**Most skiers and snowboarders complain of 'dodgy knees' from time to time. Whether they click, hurt or ache when you're asked to 'bend ze knees', you don't have to put up with it.**

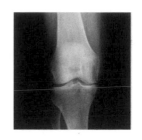

Almost 40% of all ski injuries affect the knees. From a nagging joint to a full-on snap of the anterior cruciate ligament (ACL), the knees get a raw deal in the snow.

I've blamed more than a few bad days on the piste on my dodgy knees. I'm never really sure how they got dodgy, but put in enough ski or snowboard hours and it seems sadly inevitable for most of us.

Knees are more likely to be injured on the ski hill than any other part of the body. And, when you look at what they do, it is no surprise. Not only is a knee one of the body's main weight-bearing joints, but it is also a very complex one. It simultaneously rolls, slides and rotates, while carrying your body weight at the same time.

*Here's an idea for you...*

**Hurt your knee on the hill? Elevate it, slightly bent, above your heart. Cool it steadily by covering the entire joint plus a few inches above and below for three hours with an ice compress. Compression bandaging will help any swelling. Don't take painkillers until you've seen a doctor, as they can disguise symptoms that are helpful for diagnosis.**

Part of the culprit, for two-plankers at least, is beginners' snowplough, which places huge stress on the medial collateral ligament – strains account for 20–25% of injuries. But strains are small fry when you consider the injury every skier or boarder fears most ... a dreaded tear of the ACL. This ligament inside the knee acts like an internal guy rope binding the thighbone to the shinbone, and a tear can put a question mark over any future trips to the slopes.

Up to 15% of all skier injuries are ACL tears and are almost always caused by a twisting fall. Often you'll hear a 'pop' when a cruciate ruptures, and the knee will give way, swelling within an hour. It usually happens when falling backwards with your weight over the tail of your skis. Risky manoeuvres are getting up while moving after a fall, trying to sit down after losing control and landing a jump leaning backwards.

Snowboarders escape more lightly because both feet are strapped to the board and twisting happens with the whole body, but risky times for riders are big air, flat landings and riding the T-bar.

Being a woman also ups your risk. ACL injury rates are four to eight times higher in women, according to research published in the *American Journal of Sports Medicine.* Higher oestrogen levels soften the ACL, particularly during ovulation, making the fairer sex more vulnerable. Women are also more likely to land jumps with closer together, straighter knees than men, exerting more twisting force, according to researchers at the University of North Carolina.

## SO WHAT CAN YOU DO TO PROTECT YOURSELF?

The simple answer is that your first French ski instructor was right – bend ze knees. Always keep your arms forward, feet together and hands over skis. Don't straighten your legs when you fall, and when you're down, stay down until you've stopped sliding. Don't jump unless you know how to land (keeping the knees flexed and landing equally on both skis).

Warming up properly may also help, according to a paper in the *British Journal of Sports Medicine*. Why? It seems to improve the sense of where your knee is in space, according to the medics. This may increase the sensitivity of the protective muscle reflexes around the knee, which may reduce your chances of injuring a ligament.

Popping a few pills may also be worthwhile. For many people the production of glucosamine in the body declines with age, so that cartilage loses its ability to act as a protective shock absorber. Studies suggest that glucosamine supplements can boost cartilage health and build up protection. Chondroitin is another major cartilage builder and can relieve pain and swelling by rebuilding eroded joint tissue. But the effects take time, so the earlier you start, the greater the benefit.

So what if the worst happens, and you hear that sickening ACL 'pop'? Torn cruciates can't repair themselves, but the general trend is to forget surgery and treat it with splints and physiotherapy (with the aim of building up muscle and stabilising the joint). Otherwise, if your knee continues to give way, reconstruction is the way to go, especially if you want to ski at a decent level.

Protect your pins with a proper pre-piste warm-up. Turn to Idea 17, *Body shock*.

*Try another idea…*

'*Falling in love is so hard on the knees.*'
AEROSMITH obviously know all about our love affair for snowsports.

*Defining idea…*

*How did it go?*

**Q** **I heard a 'pop' before my knee gave way – does that mean it's my ACL?**

*A* *It certainly sounds like the classic sign of an anterior cruciate ligament knee sprain. It's usually caused by a combination of twisting and bending which puts undue pressure across the knee, and internal bleeding can quickly develop within the joint. If you do hear a popping sound and feel pain in your knee, do not try and get up alone but wait until someone is there to help you.*

**Q** **Are there any exercises I can do to protect my knees while skiing?**

*A* *Yes, try these two exercises to strengthen the quads and hamstrings around the knee. While sitting, tighten the muscles around your kneecap. Concentrate on tightening the muscle on the inside and slightly above the kneecap. Hold for 10 seconds, 10 to 40 times a day.*

*For your hamstrings; with your knee slightly bent, put your heel over the edge of a chair or table. Tighten your muscles on the backside of your thigh. Think of bringing your heel towards your body but don't move, just tighten for 10 seconds. Again do this 10 to 40 times a day.*

# 20

# Get on board

**Ready to buy yourself the ultimate accessory in cool?
Do your research right and buying a snowboard could be
one of the best investments in fun you ever make.**

OK, so it looks beautiful, it's got super-
cool graphics and Terje Haakonsen rides
one ... but don't go buying your first snowboard
until you've done your research. Buy for love, not
lust.

The first time I went snowboarding, I loved it immediately. Despite the tumbles,
bruises and socks stuffed down my pants for extra padding, I knew I was hooked
for good. But still, it took me several seasons to commit to buying my first board.
Although this was down to cash flow constraints rather than design, it's actually a
good idea to hold fire on buying a board straight away, no matter how irrepressible
your enthusiasm for sliding sideways.

If you take the time to read some snowboard magazines and get some more time in
at dry slopes, it will save you time and money in the long run because your ability
changes rapidly in your first few weeks of riding. What you lusted after at the end
of week one will be very different to what you lust after with a couple of weeks'
experience under your belt.

## LOOK FOR A BOARD THAT WILL HELP YOU PROGRESS

The learning curve from total beginner to reasonable intermediate is short, but steep. You need a forgiving board when you're learning the absolute basics, but once you're linking turns a stiffer board will help as you learn to carve.

The length and flex of the board will depend on your height and weight. Women generally need a smaller board which is quite light. If you want to progress to jumping and spending your time in the terrain park, you might need a slightly more flexible board, but for carving up the mountain, a stiff board is a better bet.

*Here's an idea for you...*

**Found your dream plank? Try the board on with your boots in the bindings and check your feet aren't hanging too far over the edges. Make sure the bindings are the right size and hold your boot tightly. Above all, you should feel comfortable (if a little silly, riding carpet in May in front of all those other shoppers).**

There are basically three different types of snowboards available: Freestyle, Freeride (All Mountain), and Alpine (Carving) boards. The Freeride board is the most popular and versatile, accounting for half of all snowboard sales. You can use it anywhere – on-piste, in the park, in the pipe and in powder. Freeride boards tend to have a stiff tail and a soft nose to aid fast turns in compact snow and to help you float in the soft stuff.

Freestyle boards tend to be wider (so more stable), shorter and softer. All this means they are great at handling bumps and are easier to turn. Although they are designed to be used for tricks in terrain parks and half-pipes, they are also a good bet for beginners looking for a forgiving board. But, beware if you want to ride fast and hard – Freestyle boards have limited edge grip and stability.

Carving Alpine boards are stiffer, longer and narrower to make them stable at high speeds and to allow clean, edge-holding carved turns. As with Freeride boards, they are built to ride in one direction for racers, not for jumps, airs and tricks all over the mountain.

**The board may be what it's all about but, with snowboarding, it's your boots that you should really take time to focus on. Cruise over to Idea 30, *Keep your feet sweet*, for top tips.**

*Try another idea...*

Take advice from a good retailer and ask lots of questions about what type of rider the board would be suitable for. Most indoor slopes and some forward-thinking snowboard shops in ski resorts will let you take a board for a test ride before you commit to buying.

Buying second-hand can be a smart idea too, providing you know what to look for and the seller has looked after their equipment. Ensure that the edges of the board aren't cracked and that there is no impact damage anywhere around the board. Bindings are usually pretty sturdy and a second-hand pair shouldn't give you too many problems, with the exception of the ratchets and straps which can take some abuse. Test the ratchet to see that it still functions smoothly and holds the boot tightly. A worn strap can be simple and cheap to replace, but if the ratchets have gone, steer clear.

*'Snowboarding is an activity that is very popular with people who do not feel that regular skiing is lethal enough.'*

DAVE BARRY

*Defining idea...*

*How did it go?*

**Q    I've chosen my board – now what?**

*A    Strap in with your snowboard boots and see how well they fit together. If you need copious amounts of forward lean, check how well the adjuster works – some slip. Straps vary greatly, so strap in tightly and feel for pressure spots created by the edges, and particularly check the ratchet/ buckle. Also test the buckle for ease of use with gloves on, and for durability.*

**Q    Does it matter if I go for a 'sintered' or 'extruded' base?**

*A    Most snowboard bases are made from a polyethylene material called P-Tex and are either 'sintered' or 'extruded'. Extruded bases are melted and cut to shape. They are long lasting and easy to repair. However, the extruded type of base is the slowest and holds less wax than the other types of bases. Sintered bases, on the other hand, are first ground into powder, heated, pressed and then sliced into shape. A sintered base is superior to the extruded base – it's more durable, faster, and holds wax better. Even so, it's more expensive and difficult to repair.*

*If you're looking for high performance, opt for sintered. If you're on a budget, extruded is fine. If you want top-notch stuff look for a graphite base, which holds wax best.*

# 21

# Nailing nerves

**Whether you lose your nerve at the top of a double black diamond, or halfway down the ski bunny nursery slope, there's plenty you can do to flatten the fear.**

Everyone has an attack of the wobbles at some point in their snow career. Most of us experience it every time we ride. Here's how to kill a crisis of confidence.

Even the most gung-ho 'yo' boy has probably had something shake his confidence on the slopes at one time or another. Whether it's panicking halfway down your first black run or freezing with fear when you realise they really did mean 'experts only' when you make your first heli drop, a sudden loss of confidence is the most common skiing and snowboarding pitfall.

The confidence-sapping cycle is so common because we're all experts at feeding our subconscious negative thoughts. Most of us know what this feels like. It's those 'My buddies are so much better than me' thoughts that hit you as you make tentative turns in their tracks; the 'I'm going to make a prat of myself' worries as you drop into the half-pipe; the 'I'm going to fall on my coccyx *again*' mentality that makes you as stiff as your board. If you go around telling yourself you're rubbish, your subconscious will do everything to prove you right.

*Here's an idea for you…*

**Want to change a limiting belief into an empowering one? Rewire the negative neural track created in the brain. You do this in exactly the same way the track was created: by using self-talk or affirmations. An affirmation is a positive statement of fact or belief in the present tense that will lead towards the end result you expect (e.g. 'I am a strong, confident rider'). As you 're-programme', repeat it aloud every day for between 5 and 20 minutes.**

Your conscious mind always *wants* to help you, but it usually messes you up because you can't set it aside. Instead, you have to get it involved by anchoring it in technique. Then, your unconscious mind, working with your motor memory, will take over for you.

Psychologists and neuroscientists have established that every person carries on an ongoing dialogue, or self-talk, of between 150 and 300 words a minute. If you panic, that self-talk almost always turns negative, creating limiting beliefs that become a self-fulfilling prophecy. In other words, if you tell yourself 'don't move or you'll fall', one move and you will.

## FIGHT THE FEAR

Beliefs, positive or negative, are literally etched on the brain in comfortable grooves or neural pathways. So, have a plan of attack ready to wield against your most common negative thoughts so that you can bring them to mind easily when you need them. The only way to do this is to prepare in advance by building up a logical defence to counter each negative thought. For example, if your recurring thought is 'I'll fall on a steep run', write down why that's illogical and why reason and common sense show you *can* do it (e.g. you don't normally fall over, you are strong and fit, you have good equipment, etc.).

You need to practise, but if you do you'll be able to summon up positive thoughts to replace the bad ones in any given situation.

**Accept that a certain number of falls are an inevitable part of the learning process. Find out how to temper your tumbles in Idea 40, *Let's get ready to tumble*.**

*Try another idea…*

If you're attempting a trick or a difficult run for the first time, it's all too easy to get anxious or excited. Your heart beats faster, you breathe faster and your muscles tense. If you worry about the 'what ifs' of falling as well, your worries will join the physical changes to ruin your performance. This is called choking.

To prevent choking, you need to stop the negative loop from getting started in the first place. Take a slow deep breath from your abdomen when you feel yourself getting uptight or thinking negative thoughts. As you exhale, focus on relaxing the muscles in your neck, arms, shoulders and legs. This process is called centreing. Now re-focus your attention on what sports psychologists call 'focus cues', a tactical self-instruction directly related to the process of what you're about to ride. By focusing on the process (i.e. watch the kicker), you block out all the distracting sights, sounds and thoughts that remind you of the importance of the outcome.

**'It's really important to accept that some days, it's just not working.'**
World cup snowboard half-pipe champion, LESLEY MCKENNA

*Defining idea…*

**Q**   **I told myself a million times that I can do this, but the moment I was on the hill with my mates, I saw how much better than me they are. How can I stop obsessing about how I don't match up?**

*A*   *Don't focus on the skill of your ski companions or yesterday's wipe-out. Instead, concentrate on what you do well. When you do something good, congratulate yourself. Forget the bad runs and let mistakes wash over you. Control the controllables and forget what you can't change or control.*

**Q**   **My mind said 'relax' but my body was anxious and uptight. How can I get it to chill?**

*A*   *Your mind and body need to know what tension and relaxation feel like. Starting with your head and working down, alternate flexing the muscles in each body part (producing tension), then relaxing them. Mentally and physically memorise this feeling of relaxation and incorporate that feeling whenever you feel anxious or uptight.*

# 22

# Getting air time

**So you can cruise red runs and shred black runs in your sleep? Take it to the next level with on-piste pops and blink-and-you'll-miss-it jumps. It's the best way to prepare to get some air.**

Freestyle is the essence of modern skiing and snowboarding. Getting air, pulling tricks and generally pushing the boundaries of sliding downhill is what has brought a new synergy to the two squabbling snowsports. Fun is the name of the game, whether on one plank or two, so let's play with gravity and learn to fly.

I wasn't even aware I was doing my very first jump until I was in the air. There I was riding gently over some bumpy terrain, when suddenly I was catapulted what felt like metres in the air. In fact, it was more like a couple of centimetres, but when you're in the air it doesn't matter how high you are, as long as you're in it.

Here's an idea for you… **Buy a trampoline for your back garden and try out all the freestyle moves you'd love to be able to do on the snow. All the freestyle elite practise this way and there's no better training. Put a thick layer of tape around your edges to protect the trampoline and begin by practising spins, letting your body follow your head through the turn. Progress to grabs but remember to draw your skis or board as close to your body as you can – reaching out for your edges will only send you off-balance.**

The chances are your first jump will be off something similar – hitting a bump, building your own ramp, even hopping ollies on the flats – it's all legitimate jumping and perfect practice to get you going.

Once you've played about by skiing or riding over simple jumps like this, you can move on to the bigger stuff (yep, the stuff that will probably get you noticed).

Find something with a two to four foot drop and a clean landing. It should have a nice, steep landing and a clear, obstacle free run-out zone.

On a snowboard, finish your turns so that you hit the jump straight with barely enough speed to catch some air. Begin low and compressed with your weight centred over your board, your head up and your arms out in front of you for balance. Just before you take-off, flatten the board. Now you can either ride straight over it or, for a bit more flair, pull both knees up to level out the board once you clear the lip.

Look at the landing to stop you wobbling and reach for it with your legs. Don't wait for the ground to come to you – extend your legs and go to it. This will give you more time to absorb the landing with your knees.

Absorb the impact by bending deep at your knees and touch down quietly. Build up to larger jumps by springing higher in the air off the small stuff (stay really compressed before the jump, then pop upwards as you leave the lip).

On skis, the idea is much the same. The key is to keep perfect balance, making sure you're not too far forwards or backwards. Approach the jump straight on and compressed. As you reach the lip, push up off your legs and totally stretch out. Again, land by absorbing the impact and compressing low again.

**Now you're comfortable in the air, progress to the terrain park. See Ideas 9 (*Park life: snowboard*) and 29 (*Park life: ski*) for confidence-boosting advice.**

*Try another idea…*

## IN A SPIN

Ready to add a few style tricks? OK, skiers try the twist – keeping your head in the same direction, rotate your skis 90°. When you can do it in one direction, try the other side. Then progress to doing a twist to the left and the right in the same jump – the twister.

Boarders, try a tuck or sidekick. To do a side-kick, pretend you are kicking yourself in the backside with your board when you jump. For a tuck, do the opposite and pull your knees towards your chest. Once you get the hang of them, add a grab – just reach down and grab your board with your hand in the air. The closer you pull your board towards you, the easier it is.

**'When once you have tasted flight, you will forever walk the earth with your eyes turned skyward, for there you have been, and there you will always long to return.'**
LEONARDO DA VINCI

*Defining idea…*

97

Knowing how to jump can give your overall riding technique a huge boost. Air awareness gives you the confidence to charge down hills, cut across bumps and launch off lips. If a bump catches you out, think like a cat and always land on your feet.

**Q  I keep falling on my knees when I land a jump on my snowboard. What am I doing wrong?**

A    It sounds like you're probably jumping slightly off your toe edge. If you launched off your heel edge you'd fall the other way, onto your butt. Try to launch from a flat base by kicking the tail out a bit to slow you down, then straightening up just before you jump.
    Never try to land on an edge, it will crush your heel or toe in your boot – ouch.

**Q  I can't seem to lift myself off the ground to jump on the flats. I feel like I'm stuck to the snow with glue – why?**

A    When you're trying to ollie like this, you need to get a little bit of speed going. The key is to compress yourself into a squat, then jump up lifting your front foot (or front of your feet on skis) forwards first. This loads up energy in the tail to give you the spring you need to get airborne.

## 23

# Bend ze knees

**Feeling a bit shaky trying to master a snowplough turn? Focus on the right things and you'll find your ski legs in no time at all.**

It may look a bit ungainly, but the snowplough is a novice skier's best friend. Once you master the art of pushing your heels out, you can start to feel how the ski can work for you, not against you.

Ah, the snowplough. The ugly reason why never-been-on-skis snowboarders stick to one plank and the ultimate skier's safety blanket. But, don't knock it – once you learn how to balance properly, how and when to push against the ski to turn, you will have a skill you will rely on throughout your skiing career.

If you're anything like me, you'll be eager to bypass the snowplough, or wedge turn stage completely, and go all out to swot up on the more graceful parallel turn. In fact, several teaching methods have been designed to avoid snowplough turns altogether, but most experts agree that snowplough turns are a valuable tool in their

Here's an idea for you... **Learn to stay centred and don't rely on the front or back of your boots for too much support. Instead, balance easily over the centre of your foot and skis. Learn to push against the skis using your own muscles and feel the skis deflect you around the corner, gaining a little speed then slowing down before you want to turn again.**

own right and it makes sense to learn how to do them. Why? They teach you to use your skis independently, you'll learn better edge control and steering with your outside foot and leg. Given the choice between building good technical skiing, or quickly learning an indifferent parallel turn, it is definitely worth working on your snowplough turns.

Find a shallow slope to practise on and begin by getting a feel for the snowplough position itself. With your tips next to one another and the back of the skis pushed out, you should form a wedge or snowplough shape with the skis.

Get a feel for steering your snowplough down the fall line and allowing your weight to gently transfer to your outside ski making you turn. As you apply pressure to the outside ski to steer, dig in the edge and push against it.

Make sure your upper body stays calm and still and don't use your shoulders to yank yourself round.

Once you start moving down the fall line and transferring your weight to the outside ski, you can use the curved shape of the ski to control your speed. Modern skis are waisted, like an hour-glass. So, if you stay centred and push against the ski, it will bend, forming a curve or carved shape that sends you round the corner to turn. When you've been skiing for a while and get used to the feeling of speed, it's easy to forget this feeling of steering that you get from a snowplough turn and how the ski is actually designed to work. So it's worth coming back to the humble snowplough every now and then to remind yourself.

**Focus your mind and help fight the fear with tips from Idea 21, *Nailing nerves*.**

*Try another idea…*

It is the shape of your turn, this curve or arc, that also helps slow you down, not the actual plough itself. Once you get the hang of feeling the turn, play with rocking in and out of balance. This will help you find your centre of balance, and if you grasp this now it will make everything else you learn so much easier.

Once you've turned one way, start gliding in a snowplough position across the slope again. Steer your skis towards the fall line with your feet. It may feel terrifyingly fast as you accelerate down the slope, but try and learn to accept it – it won't last long. Sink slightly, allow the pressure to shift to your outside ski and push your outside knee forwards and into the turn. Keep pushing against the outside ski until you come right out of the fall line. As you finish your turn, rise back up into the gliding snowplough, before beginning your next turn. Try to get into a rhythm of rising to start the turn and sinking to finish.

Finally, remember that your skis are designed to turn, so let them. Start the turn with gentle steering and the rest should follow. If you find yourself jerking your upper body round to finish the turn, hold your ski poles out in front of you, parallel to the ground as you ski. This will help to keep your shoulders and upper body centred and still.

*'There is no "right" or "wrong" when sliding downhill. As long as someone is safe, having fun, and smiling when skiing or riding, then they're doing something right.'*
EARL SALINE, an American Association of Snowboard Instructors (AASI) professional.

*Defining idea…*

*How did it go?*

**Q  I keep losing my balance at the end of a turn. What am I doing wrong?**

A   *You may be relying on your equipment for balance. Concentrate on your feet in your boots, as if you had trainers on, rather than trying to balance against the equipment. Don't worry what your body looks like or is doing, just aim to stay centred by using your muscles and limbs.*

**Q  Why aren't my snowplough turns slowing me down?**

A   *'The reason for turning is to change direction,' says ski instructor Sally Champman at Inspired to Ski. 'One of the main pitfalls for novice skiers is believing that you turn to slow down! Change that perception. What you do with the skis having changed direction will then dictate how fast or slow you travel. Turn them quickly to create a skid, and you'll slow down as they turn completely across the slope. Or, push hard against the edge of the ski and you'll initially go faster before gradually turning the ski up the slope.'*

## 24

# Cool and the gang

**The best group holiday has got to be a holiday in the snow. If you've been lumbered with the legwork this year, here's the leadership low-down for planning a perfect powder party.**

Been nominated as 'group leader' this year? Yes, there may be a dozen tastes, budgets and needs to cater for but, with a little planning, playing host needn't be a hassle. Here's how to earn eternal gratitude from all.

I don't know how I manage it. But every year when the annual group ski trip comes around, I seem to get lumbered with organising it.

Maybe it's the control freak in me, but I no longer look upon this as a chore. Being 'group leader' earns you the right to make crunch decisions on where you go, stay and party, it earns you cash savings and, most of all, it earns you big-time brownie points.

## LET'S START WITH THE GOOD NEWS

If you're booking with a tour operator, most will offer the group leader (yes, that's you) a free place and a free lift pass. If you're not automatically offered this, ask, saying you understand this to be standard practice for group bookings. It is and, if a company doesn't offer it, it's worth going elsewhere.

Of course, the done thing is to share this discount between your group, reducing the amount you each have to pay. If you don't come clean about the free place to your pals, you may get found out and have some seriously miffed companions on your hands. This happened to a friend of mine whose turn it was to organise the annual ski trip. Unfortunately for him, we were all wise to the free place system and he was forced, red-faced, to come clean. You have been warned.

*Here's an idea for you...* **Not sure what type of trip to plump for? A chalet holiday tends to work best for groups. If you can take over a whole chalet, you'll have a more private 'team' atmosphere where you can share in-jokes to your hearts' content. You'll also get your meals, packed lunches and sometimes wine included, which saves you the hassle of splitting every restaurant bill.**

If you want to make the most of going in a group, be sure to book early. If you get your act together at least six months before you travel, you're more likely to get your choice of

resorts and accommodation. If you book even earlier, between 8 and 10 months before you travel, many tour operators, chalet owners and even lift pass suppliers will offer you early bird discounts too.

Shop around and compare prices. If you aren't immediately offered a group discount or early bird discount, ask anyway what reductions can be made for your group. You'll be surprised how often this will get you money off and if you don't ask, you don't get.

If you're willing to be a bit flexible on dates, you'll get the best rate. Instead of telling a tour operator specific dates you want to travel on, give them a more flexible time bracket and ask when the best deal would be. Many of the large tour operators will offer up to seven free places for really large groups (between 36 and 42 people) if you pick your time right.

**Want to know how to match your group to the right resort? Turn to Idea 41, *Perfect match*.**

Try another idea…

'*Snowflakes are one of nature's most fragile things, but just look what they can do when they stick together.*'

VISTA M. KELLY

Defining idea…

Usually 'the right time' is low season when there are fewer people on the slopes, and the prospect of filling a large number of empty beds in one booking becomes very appealing to the holiday supplier.

## DON'T UNDERESTIMATE YOUR 'TEAM LEADER' RESPONSIBILITIES

People, even if they are your best buddies, can be unreliable. They may change their minds or have events crop up that they simply can't miss. Whatever the reason, make sure it doesn't jeopardise your group plans by ensuring you can make a name change before the departure date without penalties. This applies even more so if you made your booking very early. Remember, as group leader, you are responsible. If the worst comes to the worst, you are the one liable to cover any outstanding payments.

If you booked with a tour operator and have insurance recommended by them, you may be able to claim for any losses incurred. The same is true if someone cancels for medical reasons.

Book as much as you can in advance – ski and snowboard hire, lift passes, excursions – especially if you choose to travel with a tour operator. The discounts you'll get by asking as a group will be much more than the discounts you'll get in resort as single travellers. If you booked with a tour operator, groups may also be entitled to a free ski escort, saving on the cost of a ski guide in resort.

**Q**   **I've been offered a good rate on insurance by the tour operator – shall I book for everyone?**

*How did it go?*

**A**   *Not until you've checked whether your pals are already covered. Many people take out annual policies of their own, but check everyone has insurance that covers skiing and snowboarding, off-piste if you intend to go there, loss of your kit, piste closure and, heaven forbid, no snow. It's also a good idea to photocopy any insurance documents, particularly if you're skiing stateside, so that everyone knows where to access them in case of emergency. If you're in hospital after an accident, you'll need someone else to be on the case with your insurance details.*

**Q**   **We are a group of single girls who have skied a lot before and want somewhere that will provide us with plenty of challenges – on and off the pistes! Where do you suggest?**

**A**   *If you're looking to bag a man as well as some challenging terrain, go somewhere like St Anton or Chamonix. With reputations as 'hard core' resorts, they have a much higher percentage of male skiers than other resorts. Some claim that the man:women ratio is 70:30.*

# 25

# Perfecting parallels

**Progressing from awkward-looking snowplough turns to perfect parallels is the biggest leap you'll make in skiing. It's tough, but not rocket science; it's simply about getting your mind and your body working in parallel, too.**

Parallel skiing is the Holy Grail that most skiers are desperate to search for. But the key to successful schussing is to think in curves, not in straight lines. If you link curves then parallel skiing is easy.

Just as parallel skiing and snowploughing look worlds apart, they feel worlds apart too. Before, you were learning to feel for your edges, but now the focus is on pivoting your skis and letting the curve do the work.

In theory, the first part of a parallel turn should be the easiest, because gravity is already trying to pull your skis down the hill in the direction you want to go. But as you're traversing, before starting a turn, your skis are tilted on to their uphill edges.

While you're 'holding an edge' like this, your skis actually resist the pull of gravity down the hill. To go from a traverse to a parallel turn, you need to release those edges by flattening your skis and eventually rolling them onto their opposite edges, the 'new' edges that will control the turn.

## LET'S TAKE IT STEP BY STEP

As you traverse across the slope, extend your legs and body and stand upright. This will make your skis flatten, allowing them to drift naturally down towards the pull of gravity. Once the turn is underway, roll your skis onto the new edges and drive them around the rest of the turn. Try to think of pivoting, rather than edging, your skis by imagining pivoting your feet on a large circle.

Remember that parallel lines never meet, so keep a wide stance throughout your turn and don't pull your feet together as if you were on a monoski. Keep the feeling of working the skis and legs independently of one another.

*Here's an idea for you...* **Take a leaf out of Prince Harry's book and hire yourself a pair of snowblades for a day. Because they are so much shorter they can really help your balance and teach you how to use and work with the shape of the ski. Use them with or without poles and your parallels should be easier to feel.**

As you turn, try not to worry when you feel the speed kick in around the curve. Instead, relax and enjoy it – you aren't going down the hill, you're curving around, so don't panic. Let it curve before thinking about curving back the other way – always think of linking curves, not straight lines.

Concentrate on learning to stand on your skis and steer them, rather than pushing them to make them turn. There is a subtle difference. Remember, you are the driver, not the passenger.

**Mastered the groomers? Turn to Idea 27, *Lumps 'n' bumps*, and learn how to ride the bumpy stuff too.**

Try another idea...

The problem most novice parallel skiers have (and one I grappled with for weeks) is an inability to release both edges simultaneously and tip both skis together onto their new edges. You'll generally find it easy enough to get the new outside ski (i.e. the right ski when turning left) to do it because of your snowplough experience. The problem is getting the new inside ski to do the same thing at the same time.

To master this, concentrate on steering the skis around the curve and focus on tilting the new inside foot from the 'big toe edge' over on to the 'little toe edge'.

Don't forget your pole plant. Your poles are much more important to you now you're paralleling and will help to stabilise your upper body, which, for short, rhythmic turns, should always face down the hill.

Plant your pole at the same time as you extend your body upwards to start the turn. In short turns, this will really help you to turn your skis just by pivoting your legs, instead of rotating your whole body. In long turns, it will help you to keep your upper body facing down the hill and your hips angulated into the turn, which should automatically keep your skis on edge.

*'Use what talents you possess; the woods would be very silent if no birds sang except those that sang best.'*
HENRY VAN DYKE

Defining idea...

Finally, how about mastering that showy parallel stop where you spray your waiting mates with powder? To do this, learn to pivot your skis, rotate and skid to slow down, instead of careering out of control while grappling for an edge. It is paramount that you learn to scrape off speed as you travel around your curves rather than edging, because once you find your edges, you'll only pick up speed and crash into your friends instead of slowing to a heroic halt.

*How did it go?*

**Q**   **I'm skiing with people who are better than me to give me something to mimic. Is this a good idea?**

*A*   *Probably not. It's really important to learn at your own rate rather than skiing on slopes that are too steep for you and feeling under pressure to keep up with faster skiers. Go and grab a private lesson (preferably in your mother tongue) – one-on-one tuition is the fastest way to learn. Who knows, you could be out-paralleling your pals by the end of the week.*

**Q**   **I'm miserable. Two days of this and I'm still not getting parallels – what shall I do?**

*A*   *They may look a bit more graceful than the snowplough but parallels aren't the be all and end all of skiing. It's really important to learn to snowplough properly first, and then progress to a step turn. These techniques and tools are useful for all the conditions on the mountain, so go back to perfecting the previous stage and feeling the way a ski turns before obsessing about parallels.*

# 26

# Learning to link

**So you can sideslip left and sideslip right on your board? Take it to the next stage and link those turns. This is the moment it will all 'click'. Prepare to look like a pro in days.**

Getting down the slope is one thing, but if you want to do it in style you need to link turns to trace beautiful 'esses' in the snow. It looks graceful, feels awesome and really isn't as hard as it looks.

Old school skiers with a chip on their shoulder about crazy, out-of-control snowboarders like to harp on about how skiing is so much more technical, more skilful and harder to execute well. Snowboarders usually put up a bit of a fight but, to be honest, the snooty ski crowd are probably right.

On two planks, you've got four edges to think about, you've got two independent legs to steer and you've got two poles to worry about planting. On a board, things are a hell of a lot easier. In fact, if you want to turn, there are only three basic things

113

**Chill out. Snowboarding well means keeping your body loose, relaxed and flowing so that you can absorb any unexpected lumps and bumps. For instant results, take five deep breaths from your abdomen, shake out your arms and legs and ride with renewed relaxation.**

you need to remember: look in the direction you want to turn, put your weight on your front foot and tilt the board onto the edge you're turning onto. Sounds easy? Let's try.

Before you start moving, check your stance. Keep relaxed, with knees slightly bent and hands balanced in front of you at waist height. If you're a regular stance rider, a toe side turn will mean turning right and a heel side turn means left. If you're goofy, it's the other way round.

Ready? Point the nose of your board down the fall line and put your weight on your front foot. As you pick up speed, hold your nerve, look in the direction you want to turn and begin to dig in your uphill toe edge.

As the board starts to turn, sink down, balance evenly on the balls of both feet and you'll find yourself slowing to a traverse across the hill. Allow yourself a moment to slow down and traverse a few metres across the hill. Once you're ready, extend your knees and rise up a little to unweight your board and prepare to go into a heel side turn.

Wait until your board is pointing down the fall line again before beginning to dig your uphill edge in. If you dig that edge in before your board is pointed downhill, you'll catch the downhill edge and slam hard into the snow. Ouch.

Once your board is pointed downhill, look in the direction you want to travel, put your weight on your front foot, tilt onto your heel edge and sink your knees to balance. After a short traverse, extend and get ready for the next turn.

**Think you've got turning sussed? Take it to the next level by learning how to carve in style in Idea 32, *Carve it up*.**

*Try another idea…*

One thing that helped it click for me was when an instructor told me to imagine I was a cowgirl. This had two effects (apart from making me feel like Daisy from the *Dukes of Hazzard*). One, I had to imagine I was sitting astride a horse, which kept my legs stable and my weight evenly balanced. And two, it helped me complete each turn fully. Why? The instructor told me to imagine shooting two guns directly uphill on finishing a toe side turn and shooting two guns directly downhill on a heel side turn. This had the effect of closing my shoulders on a toe side turn and opening them on a heel side turn, ensuring I went into a proper traverse after each turn.

It's a great learning technique to help you feel the feeling of completing each turn, but remember that you need to face the direction you want to go, so once you've got the feeling, return to facing the front of your board with arms balanced in front of you.

No one links turns the first time. It'll take plenty of tumbles before you nail your first turns, but persevere. Once you feel the thrill, you'll have taken the biggest step up snowboarding's steep learning curve.

*Defining idea…*

*'The day that you stop learning is the day that you start decreasing your rewards and start suffering from frustration and lower levels of satisfaction.'*
BRIAN TRACY outlines the upside of all those wipe-outs.

**Q** **I know what I need to do to turn but my mind won't seem to let me. How can I stop traversing for miles and force myself to turn?**

A *I can relate to this. When I first started I seemed to have a mental block about turning, so would traverse as far as I could get away with before the piste ran out and I was forced to change direction. Try what I did to get over it – counting. It helps you to find a rhythm that disciplines your turns. For example, as soon as you start your first turn, start counting from one to five. On five immediately begin your next turn onto the opposite edge and start counting one to five again.*

**Q** **I'm OK on the hill, but I fall over the moment a slope flattens out and I have to ride flat. What am I doing wrong?**

A *Riding the flats, or riding narrow paths, is one of the toughest skills to master. Any time you find your board flat on its base you're in a dangerous place because the tiniest of bumps will catch an edge and cause you to fall (and falling on the flat usually means a lot of legwork to get where you want to go). Instead, always try to stay on one edge or the other. You don't have to overdo it, just pressuring the uphill edge slightly is enough to keep you stable.*

# 27

# Lumps 'n' bumps

**Not every run is a smooth, corduroy couloir. Whether you're hitting off-piste lumps or mastering moguls that murder your knees, technique is all-important.**

Ready to mix it up a bit? If you're bored with cruising the flats with the crowds, head for the mogul fields (the ones with all the bumps), the cruddy off-pistes and learn to absorb.

No matter how many times I try to force myself to fall in love with the mogul field, I somehow just can't seem to muster even a whisper of lust. Nope, the big bumps and me just don't mix. But that doesn't stop me watching those who can bounce down the bumps like coiled springs with open-mouthed envy.

It has to be said, that moguls are really designed for skiers. It's tough to tackle them with style on a snowboard (although it can be done).

On skis the trick is absorption. You want to soak up the mogul with your lower body and the technique for mopping them up is almost the opposite of what you'd do on a normal slope.

Here's an idea for you... **Don't even think about trying to master moguls before you can control your speed on smoother slopes. Prepare for the bumpy stuff by imagining that a smooth piste is full of lumps and bumps, and practise how you would ride, with springy knees, centred balance and controlled speed.**

Instead of extending your legs to start a turn, flex and pull your feet up underneath you. Keep pulling them up and compressing until the halfway point of the turn and then start to extend your legs back out again, keeping your upper body at the same level the whole time. It will feel odd when you practise on a flat piste, but that's the best place to start (provided it has a decent gradient). When you take it to the mogul field it will feel more natural as you compress to absorb the bumps.

Don't worry about finding a line in bumps. Instead, concentrate on learning how to pivot your skis to turn on the bump and to scrape or skid them to control your speed as you turn. Gradually you will pick up better routes and rhythms down the bumps.

If mastering moguls takes a while to come naturally, don't worry (I still avoid deep mogul fields like the plague). But a great way to build up your confidence for the bumps is to head off into boulder fields and trees, where natural obstacles force you to turn frequently. Being able to turn anywhere at any time will provide the skills and confidence to manoeuvre yourself in tight spots like chutes and couloirs as well as in monster moguls.

## A BUMPY RIDE

Hitting the bumps on a board isn't quite as simple a formula. There are all sorts of ways to ride them – you can turn in the troughs or turn on the tops of the bumps or even traverse across the fall line and put in tight turns down the edge of the field.

But to ride them properly, you need to get into attack mode and approach them with a bit of aggression.

Stop at the top of a bump and look at your board. The tip and the tail will be hanging in the air, totally unweighted and just asking to be turned. Begin by trying to turn on the top of a bump.

Ride up to your first bump slowly and drive your back hand forward to get in a powerful, aggressive stance. Think of your legs as springs and absorb the front and top of the bump with your knees, before extending your legs to push the tip of the board down the back of the mogul into the trough. While your lower body bounces like a spring, your head and upper body should just float along level. By soaking up the bumps with your knees and keeping your upper body still, you keep your balance and keep your vision clear. The rhythm you're looking to build up is absorb, turn, extend.

If you find it tricky to make your turns on top of the bumps, try them in the troughs instead. The moguls will force you to turn and change your line frequently, so be sure to keep looking ahead and planning. Try to plan your ride three or four turns ahead, deciding where you'll turn, where you'll slow down and how you'll keep the pace comfortable and smooth.

**Ready for the next challenge? Prepare for a powder day with tips for how to ride the deep stuff in Idea 34, *Pure powder*.**

*Try another idea…*

*Defining idea…*

*'In the end, to ski is to travel fast and free – free over untouched snow country. To be bound to one slope, even one mountain, by a lift may be convenient but it robs us of the greatest pleasure that skiing can give, that is to travel through the wide wintery country; to follow the lure of peaks which tempt on the horizon and to be alone for a few days or even hours in clear, mysterious surroundings.'*

HANS GMOSER

How did
it go?

**Q**    **I mastered the compression technique on skis on the smooth piste, but the moment I took it to the mogul field, I kept falling backwards. Why?**

**A**    *You could be compressing into your turn off balance. Make sure that, as you absorb the bump and start your turn, it is your heels tucking up behind you and not your backside just sitting back. Try to stay centred and balance with your hips over the balls of your feet.*

**Q**    **I don't think I look very stylish on moguls because my back hand always seems to want to flail and trail behind me – how can I tidy myself up?**

**A**    *Your back hand is a good indicator of your mogul technique. If it's flailing around behind you like yours, it's in danger of tipping you into the back seat and onto your backside. Instead, try to really drive that back hand forwards in the moguls. If it drifts behind you, pull it back in front of you again. This keeps you in an aggressive, centred stance, and makes moguls easier to ride.*

# 28

# Bouncing back from injury

**It doesn't stop when you're laid up. Research shows that sports psychology techniques can actually speed up your recovery time. Get back on the horse.**

Worried about your muscles wasting away while you're out of action? Try tapping into a bit of sports psychology — emerging research suggests it will get you back to full strength faster and will boost your muscle strength without you having to lift a finger.

OK, so sliding on snow probably carries more risk than many other sports (chess injuries, they tell me, are rare); but an injury is never expected, never planned and definitely never welcome.

You can of course train to prevent an injury, but most of us are never prepared for our emotional response to it. My reaction to my first broken ribs was initially laughter (it was a good dinner party yarn after all), followed almost immediately by depression when I realised I'd miss out on the rest of the action on a very expensive two-week snowboard trip in Canada.

Here's an idea for you...

**Controlling your breathing can ease stress and your response to pain. When it hurts, try to breathe freely and stay relaxed. Allow your lungs to fill completely by extending your stomach as you breathe and by feeling the air move in and out of the bottom of your lungs. Visualise healing, relaxing energy entering your body as you inhale, and a release of any negative thoughts as you exhale.**

## MIND GAMES HELP

Little did I know that the way you respond to injury is important for your recovery. Injuries mean different things to different people. For a pro, an injury might be career-ending. For other riders an injury may take them away from a lifestyle or a social structure that gives them a sense of identity, accomplishment and community. And, if you're really busted, an injury can interfere with your job, study or responsibilities at home.

Research published in *The Lancet* medical journal shows a link between your psychological state and your ability to deal with illness. So, getting the right mind-set can help you get through it easier and faster.

Thinking positively is easier said than done, but these tricks can help:

- Believe that your pain and injury is something that will go away and will heal.
- Lighten up about the inconveniences caused by your injury. Have a sense of humour.
- Maintain your sense of identity and importance through other activities that help you feel good about yourself.
- Be aware of your current level of physical ability and what abilities you may have lost, then move beyond those limitations to visualise a future level of ability.
- Focus on the injured area and create a healing image and imagine the area healing. Believing in the treatment you receive is important for speeding up your recovery too.

'When you're injured, it's really important psychologically to make sure you get proper treatment and rehabilitation,' says injury veteran and world cup snowboarder Lesley McKenna. 'If you focus on rehab and getting your body 100% fit, as well as rest and recovery, you will find it much easier to get back out there again. If you are confident in your body when you return to riding, getting back on snow won't seem like such a big deal.'

**Be prepared for any injury with tips for on slope SOS. Turn to Idea 18, *Stress-free injuries*.**

Try another idea…

But the most intriguing new developments in sports psychology are the most exciting for injured skiers who are desperate to get fit again. According to the medics, it is actually possible to increase your muscle strength just by imagining it. So, if you break your leg, even though you can't physically move it for months, by playing mind games you can stop your muscle from wasting away.

In a study at Cleveland Clinic, Ohio, scientists found that simply imagining exercising significantly increased muscle strength. Ten volunteers did 'mental workouts' five times a week, imagining lifting heavy weights with their arms and increasing their bicep strength by a whopping 13.5%. Not only that, the gain in strength lasted for three months after they stopped the mental exercise regime.

Why? Mentally envisaging exercise increases the strength of the command signal sent by the brain to the muscle. Muscles are prompted to move by impulses from nearby motor neurons, and the firing of those nerve fibres depends on the strength of electrical impulses sent by the brain. If you train them, they seem to fire faster.

*'A good laugh and a long sleep are the best cures in the doctor's book'.*

Irish proverb

Defining idea…

123

*How did it go?*

**Q** **I've healed now but can't seem to muster the courage to get back out there. What shall I do?**

**A** *The first time back on the slopes after an injury can be tough. If you find that all you can think about is the accident and have reverted to side-slipping like a beginner, the best way to get over it is to start all over again.*

*Go back to the nursery slopes and go through the learning steps from scratch. In your mind, try to remember the feeling of riding well. Remember the rhythm and the movement. Before you hit the slopes imagine a colourful, exciting picture of yourself riding well and really feel it; get the good associations going again and those feelings will get you back to where you were before the accident.*

**Q** **My injury was a serious one and I can't bring myself to get back on skis, even using these techniques. Can anything else help me?**

**A** *If your injury was hard core, you could try a technique called biofeedback to get back Out There. This involves being hooked up to a heart rate monitor or something that reads your physical state. A therapist will then help you go over your accident in your mind while watching how your heart rate responds. By doing this you can work out exactly when your heart rate speeds up and which points are 'danger' zones that start a stress response. You can then learn how to control your heart rate at these points and work out what calms you down before you're actually in the situation for real.*

# 29

# Park life: ski

**It's the 21st century and skiing is cool again. Want to know what boosted its style rating? Freestyle. Yep, if you want to be a new school skier, you're going to have to get to grips with the terrain park.**

*Freestyle skiing is all about not having rules, but that's not much help when you're just trying to get started — you need help to be guided through the pitfalls.*

The first thing most people want to nail in the terrain park is jumps. It's a great place to start because it will give you a feel for getting air, and will prepare you for the more technical obstacles such as rails and the half-pipe.

Before you hit your first jump, or kicker, get used to absorbing the bumps on-piste. Try and keep contact between the snow and your skis at all times and let your body absorb the bumps.

Before you approach a kicker, or jump, in the park, talk yourself through what you are about to do. 'Rehearse jumping up and down on the spot and feel the boots flexing as you land each,' advises Warren Smith, director of Warren Smith Ski Academy (www.warrensmith-skiacademy.com). 'Then talk yourself through it.'

*Here's an idea for you...*

**Talk yourself through every jump, rail slide or half-pipe cruise before you hit them. Look at the obstacle in front of you and imagine yourself skiing up to it, compressing and popping, then smoothly and deftly carrying out the trick before sticking the landing.**

Once you're ready, ski up to the kicker as relaxed as possible. Don't do anything too early. Just hit the jump as if it were just a bump on the piste and ride over it calmly.

After you hit it, compress your body, lift your knees, keeping your weight forwards and head up. As you land, absorb the impact by bending your knees and all joints, Make sure your ski tips are pointing down so that you land at the same angle as the slope.

Easy! Now you've got the feeling of flying, progress to sliding down rails. These babies can seriously hurt if you fall, but try to remember it's just like riding on any other surface. Take it slowly and start small.

'To help you prepare for rails, try skiing with a slightly wider stance, approximately hip width apart,' says Smith. 'This gives you a better base to balance while sliding.'

Practise this lower, wider stance on the piste first for 30 minutes before taking it into the park to build your confidence.

As you approach the rail, jump smoothly onto it and position your skis perpendicular to it, with your feet shoulder width apart. Distribute your weight evenly on your feet and keep your eyes at the end of the rail. As you near the end of the rail, a small 'pop' (extend and push off) will help you clear the end of the rail and land afterwards.

## YOUR LANDING

Crash landed? So do most other skiers on their first attempt. 'The most common pitfall on rails is falling backwards with your feet slipping away from you,' says Smith. 'To avoid this happening, make sure that, as you land on the rail, you keep your weight on the front foot as well as the back.'

Right, over to the half-pipe. This is the obstacle most people tend to attempt last. And who can blame us? It's big, icy and downright scary. The good news is that it doesn't have to be. You can start in the half-pipe undaunted by simply skiing from one side to the other trying to get a feel for the shape of the pipe.

'As you get used to riding the pipe, start to let yourself flow,' says Smith. 'Don't try and come out of the top of the pipe. Spend your first day just riding and flowing with it.'

One of the common mistakes in the pipe is 'popping' too early and aggressively when you want to turn in the air. If you pop and extend with too much aggression you will throw yourself back into the centre of the pipe. It's essential to make your development a slow and progressive one here, so that you avoid getting injured. Take time with your pop and don't rush it.
Feel the flow and do it when it feels natural.

*Try another idea…*

Take your freeriding to another level by hitting the natural obstacles that are hidden off-piste. Learn how to do it safely in Idea 33, *Piste off.*

*Defining idea…*

'He who would learn to fly one day must first learn to stand and walk and run and climb and dance; one cannot fly into flying.'

FRIEDRICH NIETZSCHE

127

**How did it go?**

**Q**  **I'm falling backwards every time I hit a kicker. Where am I going wrong?**

**A**  *This is exactly what most other skiers tend to do when they start hitting jumps, so don't worry. It may be one of three things. Are you popping or extending as you go off the kicker? You need to, otherwise your body stays in the same position as the angle of the kicker as you go to travel the air, making your whole body lean backwards.*

  *Or maybe you're looking down as you travel through the air? It's a natural instinct but try to focus on and look for your landing, not your feet. Finally, it could be that you aren't flexing your ankles when you land. If your ankles don't flex it will be up to your knees, which will put your hips right over the backs of the skis. Instead, try to stomp your landing with your ankles dominating the flex.*

**Q**  **Do I need any special equipment to ski the park?**

**A**  *Yes; one of the most important things to do before you step into the terrain parks is make sure you're kitted out correctly. The essentials are a helmet, a back protector, Twin Tip skis and boots that have a nice comfortable flex. It's essential that your boots aren't too stiff and can flex comfortably so as to avoid your weight going back as you land.*

# 30

# Keep your feet sweet

**It can turn you from an average into a red-hot rider, and make or break your day on the piste. If there's one thing you need to get right before you start, it's selecting the right pair of ski or snowboard boots.**

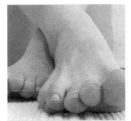

You're a European size 39, a UK 6, a US 8? Forget all that. When it comes to ski and snowboard boots, manufacturers have developed their own sizing scales, so it pays to seek out proper advice when looking for the perfect pair.

A few years ago, fitting ski or snowboard boots was as simple as selecting a slightly bigger shoe size and then padding out the gaps with a chunky pair of ski socks. No wonder that ski boots came to be seen as private torture chambers.

Thankfully, things have moved on and there are more scientific ways of making sure your feet stay happy in the snow. Nowadays, boot fitting ranges from basic heat moulding to expensive sessions with more technical gear than you'd find in a forensic laboratory.

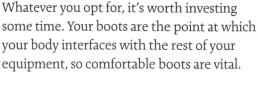

Here's an idea for you...

**Before you have your boots fitted, write a list of everything you need to tell the boot fitter. Make a note of where you ski, how long you've skied and how often you go, what terrain and conditions you prefer and which you avoid, what other equipment you use, what your skiing goals are, what your perception of the problem is and your anatomical configuration.**

Whatever you opt for, it's worth investing some time. Your boots are the point at which your body interfaces with the rest of your equipment, so comfortable boots are vital.

Get them fitted by a specialist boot fitter and allow plenty of time. Buying a pair of boots can take anything from one to three hours. Both ski and snowboard boots should fit snugly but not feel too tight. Make sure you have no heel lift, since this will affect your riding.

### FOR SNOWBOARDING ...

... look for boots with an internal lace to tighten the boot, or a custom-fit liner that can be heat-moulded to your foot. Sloppy boots make for excess heel lift that ultimately means less response, while too tight a boot means pain. If you're choosing boots for use with conventional strap-in bindings, step into the bindings because the feel can be very different once strapped in. Some people prefer a softer boot with plenty of flexibility and sensitivity, while others prefer a stiffer boot that gives their ankles more protection and their riding more stability.

Unlike snowboards, the quality of boots on the market varies hugely, especially in terms of anatomical support. It definitely pays to shop around and try on a few different pairs, even if you don't like the look of them.

Women-specific boots are definitely worth buying for the girls, as they generally have a lower cut around the calf and will feel much more comfortable.

**Tweak your body's alignment and you'll ride better, harder and faster. Find out how in Idea 2, *Find your feet*.**

*Try another idea…*

## SKIERS …

… should see a competent technician or boot fitter, who will examine both feet and both ankles, looking at how they bear weight and how flexible they are. Along with information about whether you are short, tall, long-legged, bow-legged or knock-kneed, a trained specialist should have a good idea about the kind of boot that will fit you like Cinderella's slipper.

Tell the fitter as much as you can about your feet and your posture. For example, if you spend all day chained to an office desk, you're more likely to have lower back and calf problems that affect stance, gait and balance.

**'Regular feet can't be affected by irregular shoes.'**
Chinese proverb

*Defining idea…*

131

Defining idea...

*'Give a girl the correct footwear and she can conquer the world.'*

BETTE MIDLER

You also need to be upfront about your skill level. Don't exaggerate and don't underestimate your skills. The way you ride will affect the flexibility of the boots you need.

It's also worth letting the boot fitter know about your other equipment, such as skis, snowboards and bindings, just in case any compatibility problems are lurking.

The key things to look at in your ski boot are forward lean and lateral support. Boots with more forward lean position your knee more forward over the ball of your foot and will help with balance if you're a fast, aggressive skier.

You can work out how much lateral support a boot has by squeezing the sides of the upper part of the boot. The more you can squeeze, the softer the lateral support. If you're a beginner, you'll probably need soft lateral support to allow for errors, while more advanced skiers will want more lateral support to help control their edges.

Buy your boots early in the season so you have plenty of time to wear them in – and spend much as you can afford. Forget about hype, colour and cost. It's the fit that counts.

**Q** **I've found a cheap second-hand pair of boots that fit OK – shall I buy them?**

*A* *No. Try not to buy second-hand boots if you can at all help it. Most people only sell them when they're well worn and they will have sagged to fit the shape of someone else's foot. Instead, skimp on your skis and snowboard and set aside as much as you can afford for new boots.*

**Q** **Should I wear soft boots, hard boots or hybrids for snowboarding?**

*A* *Soft boots are the most popular choice, mainly because they are the most comfortable and can be used with highback, strap bindings and flow-in bindings. If you're into freestyle or freeriding, go for these.*

*Hard boots support your foot, ankle and lower leg firmly, and are used for alpine racing and high-speed carving on hard snow, but they have to be used with plate bindings.*

*Hybrid step-in boots combine the flexible, soft upper part of soft boots and the sturdy hard soles of hard boots, and have to be used with the compatible pair of step-in bindings.*

How did it go?

133

# 31

# Steep 'n' deep

**Lovely corduroy cruisers are all very well, but if you're serious about your snowsports, the time will come when you want to push the boundaries and ramp up the incline. It may look near-vertical but, breathe deeply, you can do it.**

Your first day on the snow, that green nursery run seemed steep. Now you've progressed, steep means double black diamond, vertigo-inducing slopes. Don't worry, it's all about confidence (and a little bit of technique).

A dizzying steep can all too easily induce a severe case of the wobbles. I'll never forget the time I was 'stranded' at the top of a particularly scary-looking black run because I froze with fear. It wasn't that I didn't have the skill or the ability to ride it, I just didn't have the confidence, and that's half of what skiing the steep stuff is all about.

Here's an idea for you... **The more time you spend on steep slopes, the less scary they will seem. Even if you're not ready to carve up the back bowls yet, get yourself on those steep slopes and simply sideslip your way down. Just reaching the bottom, no matter how unstylishly, will make the slope seem less daunting next time.**

As the terrain gets steeper, the more your rational mind screams 'no!', the heavier your skis or snowboard feel and the harder it is to get into your next turn. The solution? Make your riding more dynamic and aggressive.

On skis, point your planks down the fall line so you pick up some speed. Keep low and make sure your legs are acting independently. Then, turn your feet, legs and skis across the direction you are travelling (your skis will be parallel but should turn independently of one another). This will force you into a sliding, skidding motion; as the skid slows, turn your skis back down the fall line and repeat on the other side. Don't worry about edging – your skis will automatically edge when you turn them.

Of course, the quickest, and most stylish way to change direction on the steeps is to jump turn. Coming up to a jump turn, flex your ankles, knees and hips, feel for the outer ski, check your speed and anticipate your pole plant. As you uncoil into the jump and extend your legs, push downwards on your pole to unweight the skis. Lift the heels of the skis very slightly if the slope is very steep. While you are in the air, turn your feet and skis towards the fall line. Then land softly and start to feel for your new outer ski immediately to direct your new line.

Try to focus on extending up and forwards down the hill as you start your turn. This will 'lift' your skis so that they feel lighter and turn faster. As you make the turn, plant your pole firmly into the snow and project your hips and shoulders forwards down the hill.

Extend by pushing forwards and up from the balls of your feet, as if you're about to dive into a pool. As you keep extending, the skis will leave the snow momentarily, so that you are almost jumping to turn. As you land, steer the skis across the hill as much as you need to control your speed.

## DROPPING IN

Just as jumping your turns on skis can help you tackle the blackest of blacks, so lifting your board off the snow can ease your passage down the steeps.

The drill is simple: jump to unweight your board, pivot in the air, then land on the opposite edge. Practise doing this on a more gentle incline first so that you're ready for the steeps when you hit them.

When jump turning, on one plank or two, always visualise your descent before you take the plunge. Look down the slope ahead of you and picture exactly where you're going to make your first turn and visualise how you're going to do it. As well as preparing your mind for the path you're about to take, this will also boost your confidence by 'tricking' your mind into feeling you have tackled the slope before.

**Still prone to panic on the dizzying blacks? Turn to Idea 21, *Nailing nerves*, and nail those nerves for good.**

*Try another idea...*

*'What is vertigo? Fear of falling? Then why do we feel it even when the observation tower comes equipped with a sturdy handrail? No, vertigo is something other than the fear of falling. It is the voice of the emptiness below us which tempts and lures us, it is the desire to fall, against which, terrified, we defend ourselves.'*

MILAN KUNDERA,
*The Unbearable Lightness of Being*

*Defining idea...*

Concentrate fully on your turns, building up a rhythm that forces you to make turns regularly. Attack the slope positively, not conservatively, and believe that you are the one in control. The more you think about what you're doing, the less likely you are to get psyched out by the steepness of the slope.

*How did it go?*

**Q**   **Ouch – I couldn't slow my speed on skis and took a big spill down the fall line. Why?**

*A*   *On steep slopes you need to use both legs to balance with, making sure each one works independently. You probably toppled off-balance landing a jump turn. Next time, use the top ski to balance against, even if you lean against it and have to fall back towards the slope. It's safer to do this than to tumble down the fall line.*

**Q**   **Aargh! I panicked and found myself frozen to the spot. How can I get down safely when I lose it like this?**

*A*   *Relax. If you have the basic skills needed to get down a gentle slope, you can make down a black, too. If your mind just refuses to let you turn, accept it and sideslip to the bottom. On skis, face the skis across the slope and keep a firm, wide stance. Release the edges to flatten the skis and use your top ski for support. On a board, stick to your strongest edge and flatten the board slightly to lose some height – when you want to stop, just dig that top edge firmly into the snow.*

# 32

# Carve it up

**If you really want to look the business carving down the slopes, you need to dig in those edges and send arcs of powder spraying skyward. It takes guts, but it's just a few steps from cruising to carving.**

The feeling of carving down a pristine piste is something special. It's the moment you feel filled with power, grace, confidence and completely in synergy with the mountain. Get ready to feel those edges bite.

Carving takes a lot of practice. On skis, it can take years to master, and is the evolution of parallel turns but with more speed, more edging, and more pressure.

First, you need to understand the geometry of your skis. All skis have a 'waisted' shape that, when tilted onto their edge, will carve around in an arc. Yes, skis are actually designed to carve and knowing their geometry will help you 'feel' your way into carving.

Here's an idea for you... **Carving is all about the feeling. After you've mastered it for the first time, use the power of visualisation to engender that feeling in your subconscious so that it starts to feel like second nature. Before you go to sleep, take 10 minutes to re-play a mental video of yourself carving the slopes. Remember how it felt and try to feel every part of the turn.**

A good way to start feeling your edges 'bite' is to do very open, straight turns on an easy slope by keeping your legs wide and simply pushing your knees from side to side.

The next step is to raise your speed and the steepness of the slope a notch, to create the centrifugal forces you need to carve. With your feet and knees hip width apart, extend upwards as you enter the turn to create an opposite force against the one pulling you into the ground. Push your knees up the hill and you should feel your edges bite.

As the speed and forces increase, lean your hips towards the top of the hill and steer gently. If you react or make a movement too fast it can break the carve.

The end of your turn is where the force is greatest, so fight it by aggressively pushing your bottom leg against the ground. Try and think of driving your bottom ski forward so that it is almost in line with the tip of the top ski.

## BOARDING WITH BITE

Learning to carve on a snowboard is less of a leap and should click a bit quicker. The main thing you're going to need is more speed and more aggression.

Start your turn as normal, but tweak your turn a little by getting onto your new edge earlier in the turn and flexing your knees and ankles more to tilt the board further onto the edge.

Try to think of pointing your knees and toes in the direction of your turn and really driving them through the turn. You are aiming to flex the board so that it arcs, so the more aggressively you sink into the turn, the more your board will bend and carve for you.

If your board sounds like it's scraping the snow, you're not quite there. A carving turn should be much quieter, leaving sharp, neat tracks in the snow.

What you do with your upper body depends on the style of riding you want to achieve. For technical carving turns, you need to keep your upper body upright and your back straight, so that your legs make the turn and your body stays tall and calm. But one of the greatest feelings comes from breaking those rules and carving with your body laid out on the snow instead.

As you start your turn, get as low as you can, reach all the way into the turn with your inside hand and tilt your board as high as you can so that your edge really carves deeply. You're relying on centrifugal force to keep you up, so remember, more than ever, speed is your friend.

**You've got the speed, now get the tricks. Turn to Idea 22, *Getting air time*, and take to the air.**

*Try another idea…*

'*The secret of success is learning how to use pain and pleasure instead of having pain and pleasure use you. If you do that, you're in control of you life. If you don't, life controls you.*'
      ANTHONY ROBBINS' life lessons apply to carving too – it's all about being in control.

*Defining idea…*

*How did it go?*

**Q    It feels close, but I just can't seem to get my skis to bite and start carving – do I just need more speed?**

A    *Although you need to be going at speed, choose the right gradient slope to practise on. If it feels too steep and the slope scares you, then you are on the wrong slope for practising carving. And take your time. Just because you're going fast it doesn't mean your turns have to be fast too. Take your time to allow the skis to change edges without rushing.*

*If it's still not biting, try to concentrate on using your legs independently. Think of the pedalling action you use when riding a bike.*

**Q    My board keeps slipping out from under me when I try to carve a turn – what am I doing wrong?**

A    *This is called sketching out and generally happens when your balance is off. Try to balance over your board and lean forward into the turn, not back. Think about driving your knees forward and pressuring the board to get it to arc. Use your knees to initiate the turn, putting pressure on your toes or your heels (depending on which side you're turning) to make your board carve.*

*If your board still sketches out, check your boots and bindings are tight enough. If anything is even slightly loose, it will be exaggerated when you're trying to hold that turn.*

# 33

# Piste off

**At least, that's what the mountain rescue team will be if you head out of bounds without proper know-how. No matter how experienced, you're running big risks unless you have the right equipment, companions and safety sense.**

*Lovely groomed pistes are fine, but if you're serious about snowsports, the time will come when you want to go 'out of bounds'. But don't take it lightly; off-piste means preparation.*

Backcountry boarding and skiing is the very essence of snowsports and it's what puts the 'free' in freeriding. But venturing off-piste doesn't mean you can venture off on a whim.

### YOU NEED TO BE PREPARED

Let's start with your equipment. Size matters when you're riding off-piste. Although most modern skis are designed to be able to handle off-piste terrain, the wider the ski, the easier you'll ride. The same goes for boards. To get up the speed needed to carve through the deep stuff, your board should ideally reach your nose or higher.

Here's an idea for you...

**Ready to ride off-piste? First check your insurance policy. Many will only cover you for on-piste riding or skiing within resort boundaries. If you're not covered for off-piste, call your insurance company and upgrade. Never ride out of bounds without insurance.**

Next, check your bindings are tight enough. If you're on a snowboard, set your stance back slightly so that you can raise the nose of your board above the powder and carry a mini tool for adjustments. If you're on skis, get your bindings checked before you freeride. Believe me, you don't want to spend your day hunting for a ski that's come off in deep powder.

Then, check your poles if you're on skis. Bigger baskets are better than small baskets, which can sink too deep when you pole plant in powder and set you off balance.

Right, you're almost ready, but before setting out ensure you have three essential items: an avalanche transceiver, an avalanche probe and an avalanche shovel. In the backcountry there are no avalanche patrols, so you can never be 100% sure a slope is safe. These three essentials could save your life.

Your transceiver will emit a signal that can be tracked by your rescuers to find you, or, if you're doing the rescuing, change it to 'receive' and help locate anyone caught in the slide. Just make sure the frequencies of all transceivers in your group are compatible and that all batteries work. Your probe will help you work out their exact position and how deeply buried they are. In an avalanche situation every moment matters so you don't want to dig in the wrong spot, which is why a collapsible shovel is also vital for a fast rescue.

Now you're geared up, you can plan the day ahead. Find out the weather forecast and ask the local ski patrol if they have any advice about dangerous spots or recent slides. Ask them for the number of the mountain rescue service and tap it into your mobile phone.

If you're not riding with a qualified mountain guide (and I highly recommend that you do), tell someone where you are going. If you do get stranded or trapped, you'll know someone is waiting for you and will be ready to alert mountain rescue. Finally, never ride off-piste alone. If you get into trouble, you'll be on your own. Instead, always make sure there at least three of you.

Pick your backcountry terrain carefully. The most easily accessed areas are just outside resort boundaries and, with careful planning, you can get to them by chair-lift and just a bit of hiking. Be sure to check local maps so that you know where you'll end up. If you can afford to splash out a bit, go with a snow-cat operator who will guide you to the best terrain and get you to the best runs without hiking. For the ultimate off-piste adventure though, go heli-skiing. With a chopper dropping you at the top of untracked runs, you are always guaranteed a life experience that's hard to forget.

*Try another idea...*

**The more you understand about avalanches and their causes, the better you will be able to avoid risky situations. Knowledge is safety in Idea 46, *Avalanche*.**

*Defining idea...*

'*The true skier does not follow where others lead. He is not confined to a piste. He is an artist who creates a pattern of lovely lines from virgin and uncorrupted snow. What marble is to the sculptor, so are the latent harmonies of ridge and hollow, powder, and sun-softened crust to the true skier.*'

SIR ARNOLD LUNN

145

How did
it go?

**Q   I came up against a checked flag waving just off-piste and turned back because I didn't know what it meant. Is it safe to ride?**

A   *If you see checked flags waving anywhere, they indicate an avalanche risk of three or four on the International Scale of Avalanche Hazard Rating. This means there is a high risk of avalanche, and riding could be dangerous. Always check the day's avalanche rating before heading off-piste to help you assess the potential danger. A rating of one means the risk is low, that natural and human-triggered avalanches are unlikely. A rating of five, extreme, means an avalanche is almost a certainty. Black flags will often be waving to warn you of this. Even a moderate risk of two means that although natural avalanches are unlikely, human-triggered ones are possible.*

**Q   I don't feel confident enough to venture off-piste. How can I prepare for it?**

A   *Back country riding is very different to cruising down smooth pistes. You'll often have to weave your way in and out of trees, turn suddenly to avoid rocks and ride through narrow chutes and gullies. Don't bow to peer pressure if you don't feel comfortable.*

*Instead, stay on-piste and hone your skills by taking short, calculated runs through trees just at the side of the piste. Try to look for stashes of powder where you can practise turning sharply around the trees in deep snow within the safety of resort boundaries.*

# 34

# Pure powder

**It dumped down all last night and you've opened the curtains to a few feet of freshies. Are you ready to feel the freedom of floating?**

Powder skiing or boarding is one of the purest forms of riding snow. The soft stuff is forgiving, fluffy and fabulous and can lift you to a whole new realm of riding, provided you're prepared.

Big Wednesday. Epic Friday. Mental Monday. I can remember every single one of the truly epic powder days I've ever ridden. From the fabulous feeling of freedom from floating through virgin powder fields, to the laugh-out-loud moments of being buried up to my chin in the fluffy stuff, powder days stay with you and they're what make snowsports so untouchably special.

Mind you, if you're just venturing out for your first taste of the deep stuff, you might beg to differ. Skiing or riding on powder feels utterly different from sliding down groomed pistes. To love the soft stuff, you'll need to learn to relax and ride in a whole new way.

## EARLY CALL

The most important rule for riding powder is get up early. The best start to any powder day is being there when the lifts open to get first tracks. Nothing can beat the primal feeling of being first to make tracks in the snow.

When you are at the top of the run, you'll soon find that powder snow is pretty forgiving, no matter how you ride it. If you're a total beginner, the steeper slopes will seem easy on a powder day because powder slows you down and, more importantly, breaks your fall. Even if you don't normally feel comfortable on a slope with a bit of a gradient, seek them out on a powder day. You will find it much easier to ski through the soft stuff if you have a bit of speed from a steeper slope.

*Here's an idea for you...*

**Before you start riding deep powder on a snowboard, move your stance back slightly to the rear of the board. This will help you float the nose and sink the tail deeper into the snow.**

Next, just push off. On skis, you'll need to lean back or be in the centre of your skis and turn just as you start to pick up some speed. You'll soon see how forgiving powder snow can be – just let the skis do the work for you and try to relax as much as possible. If you're fighting to turn and driving your skis hard, you'll wear yourself out in no time.

Snowboards love the powder, but again, it can take a bit of getting used to. Because it's deeper and lighter than your average snow, powder may make you sink and lose your snowboard if you go too slowly, or have a tough time standing up if you fall. Once you've dug yourself out of thigh-deep powder with your feet strapped to a board 3ft under the snow, you'll never want to make that mistake a second time, believe me.

Pick an open slope with a decent gradient for your first powder run and point your board straight down the fall line. You'll probably find the nose of your board wants to bury itself, so lean back slightly onto your back foot and let it float. Once you're floating, bounce your board gently and let your knees do the work as your upper body enjoys the float.

## SPEED IS YOUR FRIEND IN THE POWDER

You really don't want to slow to a halt in stuff this deep. Once you have enough speed, your board will start to plane on the surface instead of sinking underneath.

It only takes minimal effort to turn in powder and all your mistakes will be minimised by the forgiving nature of the snow. Just tilt from edge to edge gently to make turns and let your board do the work as it surfs through the snow. Once you get used to the feeling of floating, head for a steeper slope and make more exaggerated turns so that you begin to bank and send up a spray of snow on each turn.

**Now you know how to ride it, head for one of the world's epic resorts and try it out. Turn to Idea 36, *Epic escapes*.**

*Try another idea…*

*'Powder snow skiing is not fun. It's life, fully lived, life lived in a blaze of reality … This overflowing gratitude is what produces the absolutely stupid, silly grins that we always flash at one another at the bottom of a powder run. We all agree that we never see these grins anywhere else in life.'*

DELORES LACHAPELLE

*Defining idea…*

149

*How did it go?*

**Q    I keep falling backwards – why?**

A    *When you move from piste to powder on skis, you may find your shoulders become a problem. On-piste you tend to stand with rounded shoulders to aid a dynamic stance. But if your shoulders are rounded in powder or off-piste terrain, they can put you out of balance. If your shoulders are forwards when you try to absorb the shocks of the ever-changing terrain beneath the powder, no matter how much you try to take the shock with your legs, your shoulders will hurl your whole body forwards and you'll eat snow.*

**Q    Is it worth investing in a pair of fat powder skis?**

A    *Not unless you live in a resort that gets regular dumps of powder, no. It may pay to hire a pair on a really big powder day, but generally powder can be skied on all types of ski. Longer skis are harder to turn but the extra speed in the powder always makes it fun, while rapid turning smaller skis are great in steeper powder runs and for jumping in the powder.*

## 35

# Winning the mind game

**In any sport, 80% of performing well is in the mind. If you've ever been psyched out by a near vertical drop, choked before your first jump or had a mental block over something as seemingly simple as turning ... read on.**

The zone. Everyone knows it. It's that realm of riding in which everything comes together and you feel lifted to a level in which limits seem to fall away. Learn how to find your Zen zone.

You may have thought it was down to the weather, who you're riding with or whether you got lucky last night, but scientific research is beginning to reveal that there are more reliable, more predictable ways of hitting that Zen-like zone. And a sure-fire way of reaching it every time you ride is to deposit a bit of sports psychology in your mind bank.

You can train your muscles to peak fitness all you want, but muscles are controlled by nerves that have 'memory'. To improve your skiing or snowboarding reflexes,

Here's an idea for you... **Take a daily dose of powerful visualisation in the run-up to your ski or snowboard holiday. The more frequently you practise, the more likely you are to create the neural pathways needed to ride confidently. Take 10 minutes every day to imagine yourself being your best.**

you need to lay down, modify and strengthen these neural pathways. Some of the pathways (in the nerves of the body and spine) can be trained physically, but those inside the brain can be trained without moving a muscle, using sports psychology techniques such as positive visualisation and affirmations (yes, that means imagining yourself ruling the pistes and chanting stuff like 'you're the man', over and over).

When you imagine something, you create neural pathways in the brain so that when you are in that situation you naturally do it – it's as if you have done it before. Your brain can't tell the difference between what's real and what's imagined.

It may sound like crazy self-help babble, but techniques like this are used all the time by world-class athletes, business gurus and some of the most successful people around. David Beckham pictures himself scoring before he attempts a goal, golfer Jack Nicklaus imagines the flight and trajectory of the ball before he hits it. You can imagine your perfect line, too.

With imagery you can create a memory plan in your brain with inputs from your imagination rather than from your senses. You need to do it well in advance though, so that it can be readily recalled to mind when you need it. Training your mind like this means you are prepared so that if negative thoughts creep in, you can respond to them competently and confidently.

## HOW DO I DO IT?

Use imagery as a substitute for real riding, and it allows you to ski a slope you have never experienced with the feeling that you have been there before and already achieved your goal. As well as giving you a confidence boost by seeing yourself shredding the perfect line, visualisation also helps to slow down complex skills so that you can isolate and feel the correct movements of a trick or race before you drop in.

'Programme' yourself by closing your eyes and picturing yourself as the star of a film. Imagine a cinema screen, and watch yourself skiing or riding the perfect run. Imagine the colours, sounds, smells and emotions and, as it crescendos and you experience the fantastic feeling of performing at your peak, 'anchor' the feeling by clenching your right fist as hard of you can.

Next, replay the same all-action film in your mind, but this time don't watch it – imagine yourself actually in it. Again, imagine every feeling and detail, making everything as bright, bold and wonderful as possible. When you reach the peak of riding perfection, clench that right fist again. If you practise this often enough before you reach the slopes, by clenching your fist you can recreate those same positive feelings, helping you to really ride at your best.

*Try another idea…*

Tap into sports psychology when you're laid up through injury. Idea 28, *Bouncing back from injury*, lets you in on special techniques that can actually speed up your recovery.

*Defining idea…*

'Twenty years from now you will be more disappointed by the things you didn't do than by the ones you did. So throw off the bowlines. Sail away from the safe harbor. Catch the trade winds in your sails. Explore. Dream. Discover.'
MARK TWAIN.

**Q    I can't get past my mental block about jumping. How can I stop
myself choking every time I try?**

A    *By being outcome-focused ('I want to be able to tackle the big kicker'), you
can easily lose sight of the process. By breaking it down into smaller steps
and a series of goals, you'll shift your focus and stop getting blinded by
the end goal. So, if you want to hit your first jump, stop obsessing about
the kicker itself and break it down into smaller goals. First, perfect ollies
on the piste; then move onto hitting any small lump or bump you can jump
off; next, move onto just riding smoothly over a small kicker without even
trying to get any air, before finally focusing on your end goal.*

**Q    I've done all the visualisation but when I still can't do something
I get myself so frustrated that my bad mood wrecks my riding.**

A    *Smile! Sounds simplistic, but the body affects the mind too. Research from
Clark University in the US found that smiling, even if you feel angry,
actually makes you feel happiness. Why? Smiling and laughing sets off
biological processes that make us feel good. They increase the flow of
blood to the brain and change the level of oxygen, the level of stimulation
of the brain's messengers, or neurotransmitters.*

# 36

# Epic escapes

**Some ski resorts defy criticism with perfect pistes, awesome après-ski and a large dose of the X-factor. If you ski them only once in your life, it'll be worth it.**

Whistler, Chamonix, Jackson Hole, St Anton, Zermatt/Verbier … these are the classic, regal resorts of the world. Here's the inside info on the Famous Five.

### JACKSON HOLE, WYOMING

Jackson Hole is like a magnet for the hard core. Officially 50% of Jackson terrain is rated expert, and the 10% classed as beginner terrain is probably an exaggeration.

High-alpine bowls rise above tree-lined, rocky ridges, hiding some of the most challenging terrain on the planet. The most infamous in-bounds descent is Corbet's Couloir, a steep, rock-lined gash plunging through the cliffs below where you might have to jump as much as 25ft before making your first turn. Although it's not all this scary, Jackson isn't a resort for skiers looking for perfect pistes.

**Insider tip** Want to build up to the big stuff slowly? Head for Gros Ventre, a long run that steadily drops 2,700ft and is one of the best intermediate runs in North America.

## CHAMONIX

Chamonix is the extreme skiing centre of the world. And, in the shadow of Mont Blanc, the scenery is equally extreme.

If you're an expert skier looking for a challenge, you'll love it. The possibilities are enormous (so is the 2808m vertical drop) and you'll find scores of pros making their home here. If you're a novice you may be less enamoured, because apart from anything else, the lift queues can be huge.

People come here to live and breathe the mountains. It is the birthplace of mountaineering and its residents have come here to be part of it and to push the boundaries further.

*Here's an idea for you...* **Picked your classic? Now get inspired with some classic mountain literature. Read *The Mountains of My Life* by Walter Bonatti – a series of narratives of classic mountain experiences.**

*Insider tip.* On sunny days intermediates should head straight for south-facing Le Brévet, where the snow seems to turn to corn and the views of the Mont Blanc massif are the best.

## WHISTLER, CANADA

Whistler-Blackcomb is a ski area of superlatives. The biggest ski area in North America (boasting more than 7,000 acres of skiable terrain), the most efficient lift system and, an accolade it receives with amazing regularity from the voting public, the 'best ski resort in the world'.

It's not hard to see why. Only two hours from Vancouver, Whistler is everything to everyone. The skiing is great for all abilities, from pro to beginner, and the off-piste with couloirs and bowls provides some of the best powder around.

The town buzzes with an international atmosphere and has facilities that knock the socks off most other resorts – world-class restaurants, lively nightlife and every kind of accommodation from five star luxury (like the impressive Fairmont Chateau Whistler) to budget bunkhouse.

*Insider tip.* If you like steep couloirs head for Blackcomb; if you prefer powder bowls, make tracks for Whistler Mountain. If you fancy a taste of the backcountry without having to worry about safety, drop into Flute Bowl, which is patrolled but not pisted.

*Try another idea…*

**Picked your resort? Now pick a place to stay. If you want a heady taste of alpine luxury turn to Idea 39, *Hip hotels and chic chalets.***

*Defining idea…*

**'The one thing I wanted most in skiing was adventure. Adventure as in steep, long runs … powder up to my armpits … the call of the mountain wild … high alpine vistas of searing, unsullied beauty. It is alluring, addictive stuff this business of adventure.'**

PETER OLIVER

157

## ST ANTON, AUSTRIA

Known as much for its nightlife as its terrain, St Anton has a youthful, party atmosphere.

St Anton gets more snow than pretty much anywhere else in the Alps. The off-piste there is limitless, with wide-open bowls, steep chutes, long runs and consistently fabulous snow. The area is huge – 85 lifts and 250 miles of marked runs. Unmarked runs account for even more. Ski touring is also popular here and if you're ready to hike into the mountains, the possibilities are endless.

*Insider tip.* After a storm, hire a guide and head straight for the untracked summit of Valluga. It's the crown jewel of St Anton and is all above the tree line, offering everything from vast mogul fields to steep powder runs.

## ZERMATT, SWITZERLAND

It may not have the extreme terrain of Jackson Hole or Chamonix, but Zermatt is one of the most perfect, complete ski resorts, all wrapped up in chocolate-box-pretty packaging.

Completely car-free, Zermatt oozes charm, has amazing mountain restaurants, a cosmopolitan crowd, excellent nightlife and very varied skiing (394km of pistes). In short, Zermatt has something for everyone, which makes it one of the most perfect all-round resorts.

*Insider tip.* If you're a gourmet, head for Le Corbeau d'Or for the best food in town.

**Q    I can't afford high season prices; how late can I ski Whistler?**

*How did it go?*

A    *While most ski resorts close down by mid-April, there is still great spring skiing and riding in Whistler well into June when prices plunge. After that, Blackcomb Mountain opens for summer glacier skiing and riding when you can often snap up even better bargains.*

  *The trade-off is the conditions. In late season, the snow begins to melt on the lower portions of the mountains and you can no longer ski all the way down to the valley. Milder temperatures bring softer snow conditions too, but if you're a beginner this could be a bonus!*

**Q    This lot are certainly classics, but where's the most 'extreme' destination?**

A    *You could debate this one for hours. Some would include Chamonix, Jackson or Whistler from our top five, but for me, it's got to be the Chugach mountains in awesome Alaska. Just north of ski resort Valdez, this is limitless heli-riding territory. Slopes too steep to ski anywhere else are skiable here as the snow is less prone to sliding. If you come heli-riding here, expect to cover 20,000 vertical feet in a day.*

# 37

# Ssh! Snowsports' hidden gems

**Sick of lift queues and bored of busy pistes? There are still some hidden gems out there just waiting to be skied. Just keep quiet about it.**

Have you ever felt a sense of deja-vu when the annual ski trip comes around? Same old lifts, same old Euro pop in the mountain cafes, same old icy black run back to base (why do they always do that?). Open your eyes and head off the beaten track. Dream, discover, explore.

How great would it be to return from your next ski trip with a real story to tell? 'I rode the Vallée Blanche'. Sorry, been there, done that. 'I saw in New Year in Vail'. Very nice, but so did we, three years ago. 'I named a first descent in Greenland'. Eh? Now that's more like it.

There is something uniquely satisfying about taking the path less travelled and discovering somewhere new.

## THE WORLD IS YOUR OYSTER, SO GET OFF THE BEATEN TRACK

So where first? Let's start with the aforementioned jaw-dropper, heli-skiing in Greenland. I first heard about this when a snowboard pro pal of mine returned wide-eyed and with renewed lust for sliding sideways from an epic trip there. A few years ago when he was high on the tales of first descents, Greenland was an experience reserved for the privileged few. But now, it's becoming more accessible to all. A quick web search will reveal tour operators who specialise in first descent packages, and you can fly direct from Copenhagen, Iceland, Ottawa and Montreal. If you go, your runs will average 4,000 to 6,000ft of vertical drop, jaw-dropping scenery and terrain no one else has ever touched. There are three ski resorts in Greenland; Aasiaat, Maniitsoq and Sisimiut, but the best terrain is accessed by helicopter.

*Here's an idea for you...*

**Val d'Isère and Tignes get all the holiday crowds, so head for the uncrowded village of Sainte Foy, just minutes away. Here, three chair-lifts rise one after the other from 1550m to 2620m accessing Ste Foy's immense bowls and sheltered, untracked slopes.**

Of course, heli-skiing tends to be pretty amazing wherever you do it. Its very essence lies in finding untouched gems, but it can be prohibitively expensive. That's why Baqueira-Beret, a little-known resort in the northern Pyrenees in Spain with the cheapest heli-skiing in Europe, makes my list of hidden gems.

Another more cost-efficient way of accessing hidden stashes of virgin powder fields is to go snowcat skiing. Two of the best priced and little known places to do it are Grand Targhee in Wyoming and Fernie in Canada. In Grand Targhee, the snowcat ski area rivals the size of the 2,000 acres of lift-served piste. Meanwhile Fernie's gentler tree runs are spectacularly beautiful and, as a young resort, the pisted terrain of linked bowls remains crowd-free. For snowboarders particularly, who will love the natural bowls and gullies, Fernie is about as close as it gets to perfect.

**Brush up on your avalanche awareness in Idea 46, *Avalanche*, and you can explore even more remote spots.**

*Try another idea...*

Just up the road (in Canadian terms) is Kicking Horse, one of the world's newest resorts. But its tender age of two hasn't stopped it already amassing a passionate following among pioneering snowsports enthusiasts. The terrain is nearly twice the size of Breckenridge, and is rapidly expanding. The one drawback of a resort in its infancy like this is that there is little mountainside accommodation and few facilities, so visitors have to stay in the nearby valley town of Golden.

Sticking with the northern hemisphere, Sweden has to be one of the most under-rated places for alpine riding. Yes, you may think it's just flat and dark, but actually the resorts of Åre and Riksgränsen are true hidden gems. Although family-friendly Åre still has far too many slow drag-lifts, the sheer beauty of the place and the almost magical quality of the light make it an amazing winter destination with some truly excellent skiing. Meanwhile Riksgränsen, in the very far north, has already made it onto the list of 'must-ride' snowboard destinations, regularly playing host to the Arctic Challenge and offering riding under the midnight sun well into June.

*'And above all, watch with glittering eyes the whole world around you because the greatest secrets are always hidden in the most unlikely places. Those who don't believe in magic will never find it.'*

ROALD DAHL

*Defining idea...*

*How did it go?*

**Q**  **I've heard about some of the up and coming new Canadian resorts like Kicking Horse and Fernie, but I'm worried they'll be too small for a two-week holiday. Am I right?**

**A**  *Not necessarily – it depends on your level. Fernie certainly has stacks of terrain to keep the confident intermediate happy for two weeks, especially if you love bowls and tree riding. Kicking Horse is smaller, but rapidly expanding. In Canada terms the two are next door neighbours, about three or four hours' drive apart, so you could happily combine them and take a two centre trip. Many tour operators now offer this package or, if you are booking independently, you could even tie in other resorts such as nearby Panorama, south of Kicking Horse and north of Fernie.*

**Q**  **How do I find out more if these gems really are 'hidden'?**

**A**  *This is where the Internet comes into its own. Using this idea as an ideas generator, type in your destination and 'ski' into a search engine and see what comes up. It's also a good idea to contact the tourist office of the country concerned and they can do the legwork for you. Uncovering a hidden gem is certainly more hassle than a package ski trip, but it's a whole lot more rewarding.*

# 38

# Peak performance

**Stop! Before you reach for that morning croissant or plate of frites, learn that the fuel you put in your furnace makes a massive difference to your performance on the slopes. Know what to eat and when.**

Fresh snow, a blue-sky day and only a few precious days of your ski holiday left ... who needs to waste time on breakfast? If you want to ski or ride at your best, you do.

The average recreational athlete (yes, you're the athlete) needs at least an extra 1,000 to 1,500 calories a day, so it's vital to begin your ski day with at least something in the tank. The right food and drink choices can give you better endurance, more energy and prevent muscle cramping. But, sorry, that's not an excuse to pre-order a fatty full English and carbo-load on chips. You're an athlete now and it'll pay to take a leaf out of their nutrition books.

Breakfasting on food heavy in starchy, complex carbohydrates (bread, porridge and fruit, for example) provides the type of fuel you need for the start/stop action of

Here's an idea for you…

**Drink more water. It's easy to forget how much you are losing in sweat when it's cold because you just don't feel it. But once you start getting dehydrated, you start making silly mistakes. The brain is 75% water and even moderate dehydration can cause headaches and poor concentration. Once you start feeling thirsty you're already well on the way to being dehydrated, so carry a neoprene-covered hydration pack for hands-free sipping and don't wait until you do.**

downhill. Complex carbs will give you sugar for energy and fibre, but the sugar is released into the bloodstream slowly, so you can keep going for longer.

'A typical continental breakfast that you find in most European resorts is ideal,' says Jane Griffin, sports dietician and adviser to GB Olympic teams. 'Go for bread rolls plus jam, or a small bit of cheese or lean meat for instant energy and to make your meal more interesting. Avoid eating a lot of fatty food – like a big fry-up – because your body takes a long time to digest it, which can make you feel sluggish and tired.'

If you're stateside, choose a toasted bagel with jam or peanut butter, or a waffle with maple syrup.

Take high-energy snacks in your pocket or backpack so you can refuel on the chair-lift throughout the day. One of the best portable snacks is dried fruit. A handful of raisins or died apricots gives you instant energy to keep you going. And dried fruit isn't bulky and won't squash. If you can't stand dried fruit, pack a few fruit gums made with pure fruit juice – the high sugar content will give you pure energy when you're flagging towards the end of the day. The sharp taste also refreshes the mouth.

If you're thinking of your waistline, don't worry too much. I always seem to eat and drink for Britain when I'm away on the slopes, yet strangely never seem to put on weight. The reason? Snowsports are among the most energetic sports around and in the cold you burn up more calories anyway. An 11-stone skier putting in moderate effort will burn 413 calories an hour; if you're really shredding the slopes, it's more like 546 calories an hour, so you can afford to eat more than usual.

**What you munch before your holiday matters, too. Find out why in Idea 10, *Après-ski angels*.**

*Try another idea…*

The demands of your afternoon on the hill dictate how big a lunch to eat. If you're planning on riding deep powder until sunset, you need to eat carefully. Go for carbs and avoid anything that looks heavy or fatty. Go for a thick soup and roll to start and then have a light pasta dish, ideal with a bit of protein like fish or chicken. Chips are out – all that fat will weigh you down. Also steer clear of alcohol as it encourages water loss, decreases body temperature and slows down your reflexes.

If you're riding on a sub-zero white-out day, the best 'warm-up' foods include warm carbohydrates, such as oatmeal or chilli, as well as warm fluids such as hot cocoa, and steaming soup. The warm food, added to the thermogenic effect of eating, will have you toasty in no time. When you eat cold foods, your body just tries to conserve heat by reducing the blood flow to your skin surface, especially to your hands and feet.

*'All happiness depends on a leisurely breakfast.'*
JOHN GUNTHER

*Defining idea…*

167

How did
it go?

**Q  I overdid the après-ski and I all I feel like is a fry-up – will that
help me on the slopes?**

A  *Sorry, but all that fat ain't going to get you much further than the
gondola. Instead, grab a large glass of apple juice to stimulate the
digestive system and smear some honey on a bread roll. Honey is a great
pick-me-up because it contains a mix of natural unrefined sugars and carbs
that are quickly absorbed into the bloodstream. Try mixing 2tbsp runny
honey with 150ml orange juice and 150ml natural yogurt for the perfect
pre-piste cocktail.*

**Q  Are sports energy bars a good idea to take up the hill?**

A  *Yes, these bars are generally high in carbohydrate and can be a conveniently
packaged, quick and easy way to top up. They are designed to boost blood
sugar levels during endurance exercise, so if you're riding the hill all day,
they are perfect to keep you going. Other bars contain protein, often in the
form of whey casein or soy protein, and are best eaten after you've finished
for the day, together with some carbohydrate, such as a banana, to boost
your recovery. Just don't take that banana in your backpack – one wipe-out
and it'll be mush.*

# 39

# Hip hotels and chic chalets

**Few sports do classy as well as those on the snow. From apartments in Aspen to five star zzz's in Zermatt, these are the places to go if you want a taste of cold weather chic. James Bond, eat your heart out.**

It's not just the chocolate-box chalets that get hearts racing in ski resorts. A new crop of urban, ultra-cool hangouts are tempting riders off the slopes early too. Better start saving now.

Let's face it, floor-to-ceiling windows are always going to work in a ski resort. Aside from the snowsports, the scenery is what we all go for.

That's why the new boom in hip ski hotels is so exciting. Why stay in a boring purpose-built place when you can stay in a serene dream? Ah, the price, I hear you cry. Well, if you pick well, you can even do James Bond style on a budget.

The first *über*-hip ski (or, strictly speaking, snowboard) hotel to open up the Bond market to those with a budget slightly smaller than MI6, is the Riders' Palace in

**Can't afford the real thing? Turn your hotel or ski apartment into a boutique haven by taking a few touches of your own. Pack a luxurious bubble bath (to ease those aching muscles), some favourite chocolates (to lay on your pillow each night) and a lavender-filled eye patch (to woo you into the land of nod).**

Laax, Switzerland. Built with vast slabs of concrete, using funky lighting to add texture and effect, this place is pure minimalism. Each of the rooms in this hi-tech hotel has PlayStations, advanced sound systems, Internet access and videos, while suites also have plasma TV screens. There are bunk-rooms for those really counting their pennies, but it's only really the suites that are expensive. At weekends, top international DJs, live bands and dance acts spin their stuff at the Ministry of Sound-run Palace Club.

Neighbouring Saas Fee is another laid-back Swiss snowboarders' hotel, where a piano hangs suspended from the ceiling, black and white cowhide covers the furniture and banks of computer screens line the walls as in Riders' Palace; bedrooms are sleek and simple with plain pine floors and white eiderdowns, and of course, the obligatory PlayStation and CD players.

Another cutting-edge place to rest your head as you drink in floor-to-ceiling mountain views is Hotel Madelin in Ischgl, Austria. It may sound quaint and cutesy, but it's anything but. Just 100m away from some of the country's best runs, its simple, clean Zen lines contrast with the grandiose mountain scenery perfectly. Each room has a special feature so that you can take your pick depending on the type of atmosphere you're after. The 'fire room' is perfect for cruel days, a pure chill-out space to watch the fire dance. For those who prefer to chill out by being pampered there's an amazing spa and super-relaxing pool.

Not far away in St Anton, you'll find Hotel Lux, another light, airy bastion of minimalism. Each of the 26 rooms look like glass cubes and have floor-to-ceiling windows, modern art on the walls and chic modern furniture.

**You'll have to start saving if you want to afford any of this lot. Turn to Idea 4,** *Cheap thrills***, and work out how to do it on the cheap this year so that you can splash out next.**

*Try another idea…*

Stateside, there are also plenty of luxurious winter gems. Amangani in Jackson Hole, US is a huge departure from the town's traditional cowboy-style accommodation. Built on a ridge overlooking the spectacular Tetons, its sleek construction of glass, wood and sandstone houses vast halls, grand staircases and exposed brickwork. But, with faux bear-fur cushions and chamois leather chairs, you won't get chilly.

America's home of luxe skiing, Aspen, is also home to a fair share of hotels that Moneypenny would have killed to stay in with James. The Sky Hotel is a luxuriously oversized place that makes you feel like Alice in Wonderland. Everything here is over the top, from the quilted white headboards to the faux fur throws and bottled oxygen in the mini bar.

But for the real, luxury mountainside retreat, head for the Alps, to the Eagle's Nest, a chic retreat that sits above Val d'Isère's legendary La Face run, offering guests spectacular views of the awesome mountain tops above and the cosy Alpine resort below. Built from hyper-expensive reclaimed timber, this 12-person ski chalet redefines the winter package holiday. With 650 square metres of space spread over four floors, it's the ultimate in luxury living. Added extras include a swimming pool, a sauna, a pop-up plasma screen TV, a cutting-edge sound system and a chef.

*'Give me the luxuries of life and I will willingly do without the necessities.'*
FRANK LLOYD WRIGHT

*Defining idea…*

**Q**   **Minimalist chic and urban cool is all very well, but isn't it a bit boring? Where can I go for something chic but altogether different?**

A   *If sleep isn't high on your list of priorities, try the amazing Hotel California in Cervinia Champoluc, Italy. It's a music hotel dedicated to legends such as Bob Dylan, Elvis and the Doors. Each room is named after a music legend and starts playing their music on a state of the art sound system as soon as you switch on the lights. The Doors, Janis Joplin and Bob Dylan and Crosby, Stills, Nash & Young all have rooms named after them. The music theme continues into the rest of the hotel, where there is a jukebox and a night-club downstairs.*

**Q**   **Fine, until I saw the prices. Some of these 'hip hotels' are impossibly dear – how can I do it cheaply?**

A   *Pick the time you travel carefully. You're unlikely to get deals on hotels like these unless you go well into low season. That means December (before Christmas though) and April. If there's a glacier nearby of course, you could always do your ski trip in summer and catch the cheapest rates of all.*

## 40

# Let's get ready to tumble

**There's an unwritten rule in snowboarding – thou shalt fall over 500 times before sliding sideways 'clicks'. Sorry, we don't make the rules, but we can help you make it click faster.**

Learning to snowboard, especially if you're already a confident skier, can be a demoralising, humbling and frustrating experience. The good news is the pain is short-lived, the learning curve is steep and the rewards ... wow.

Snowboarding is one of those sports that effortlessly manages to look cool. If you've never stepped on a board, you imagine it must take years to get to the level of being able to carve perfect esses. But it doesn't. This is one of the greatest things about snowboarding ... you can get good very quickly.

It may seem impossible to believe at the end of day one when your arms are ready to drop off from pushing up on them to stand, and your butt feels like you've been off-roading all day in a tractor, but it's true.

Are you goofy or regular? If you're goofy, you ride with your right foot at the front of the board; if you're regular your left foot leads. Find out by pretending you're taking a run-up to slide across an icy pond – which foot would you lead with?

## BEFORE YOU HIT THE SLOPES

So what makes it click? First and foremost, your state of mind. Snowboarding is very much a mental sport – how you feel affects how you ride. If you're stiff, scared and resistant, you'll be hitting the deck in no time. Instead, begin with a light-hearted acceptance that you'll go with the flow. Accept that you will fall as part of the learning process.

Play around with your board, getting used to how it feels on the flat. Find your balance by crouching down and standing up using just your knees. Experiment by leaning over your front foot, then your back.

## AWAY YOU GO

Now take it to a gentle slope. Experiment with your edges – dig your heels in to feel your uphill edge, then sit down, roll over onto your belly and stand up on your new uphill edge. This is also how you will stop. Whenever you want to stop turn your board across the slope, tilt the board onto the uphill edge (dig your heels in on your heel side, toes on your toe side) and balance evenly over both feet.

Get used to controlling the board by sideslipping. Start off on your toe edge, facing the hill. Dig your toe edge in using your knees and ankles, so that you're on the balls of your feet, then gently drop your heels to flatten out the board and release the edge. You will begin to slide down the hill but don't look down, keep your head up and feel your balance. To slow down or stop, just dig your edge in harder. Try the same thing on your heel side. Whatever you do, don't flatten the board too far and let the downhill edge catch the snow – if you do you'll be in for a slam.

Now you've got board control, try your first glide. Point the nose of the board down the slope, lean slightly forward and put more weight on your front foot. You're snowboarding!

Once you've tried going straight a few times, try traversing left and right. By doing this you can zig-zag down the mountain without actually turning – instructors call this falling leaf.

Pick an edge, either toe side (facing the mountain) or heel side (with your back to the mountain) then look in the direction you want to travel in. Move your weight onto your leading foot and you'll start moving. Remember to stay on your uphill edge all the time. To traverse back the other way, shift your weight towards the new leading foot and look where you want to go. When you travel in the direction of the tail of your board, you're riding 'fakie' or 'switch' (backwards). You're doing it for ease of learning now, but when you do it later on, especially in the park, you'll be doing it because it's cool.

**Want to ease the 'ouch' factor from all those tumbles? Check out Idea 7, *The protection racket*, and find out how to fall safely and how to protect yourself from the pain.**

*Try another idea...*

*'I now realise that the small hills you see on ski slopes are formed around the bodies of 47-year-olds who tried to learn snowboarding.'*
DAVE BARRY

*Defining idea...*

*How did it go?*

**Q   I'm fine when I have both feet on the board, but as soon as I try to 'skate' I fall over. Any advice?**

A   *Walking with your front foot buckled to your board takes as much practice as full-on riding. Unless you misspent your youth riding around on a skateboard, or you're incredibly pigeon-toed, this won't feel natural. Lean your weight over your front foot and take your first step – just imagine you're skating on a scooter. Keep your weight over the front foot, the nose of the board pointed forwards, the base flat and take small controlled steps to skate the board forward. Try skating with your loose foot on both sides of the board and practise as much as you can.*

**Q   I think I've got my legs and body sorted, but without poles what do I do with my hands?**

A   *Snowboarding is all about balance. If your arms are out of control, they will throw you off. Ideally your arms should stay comfortably flexed around waist height and just in front of you in a balanced position. When you're learning, try letting your front hand hover over the edge you're about to turn onto, to help direct your turn. If you're turning onto your toe side, move your hand over the toe edge and vice versa. This closes your shoulders on toe side turns and opens them on heel side turns to get you into the right position. This helps in the early days, but essentially, you're aiming for a neutral balanced stance at all times.*

# 41

# Perfect match

**Is your chosen resort lively? Did you get it at bargain basement price? Is it in with the 'in' crowd? Forget all other criteria, there's only one comparison that really matters: match your resort with your ability and you'll get it right every time.**

If you love the mountains, it's hard to have a bad snowsports holiday. But my most mediocre trips have been to resorts that just didn't match up to my ability. Don't make my mistake — do your research before you go.

Most resorts claim to offer something for everyone, but try telling that to a novice who's stranded at the top of a black trying to access the blues below. No, some resorts are more beginner-friendly, others cater more for those who want to be challenged (or terrified).

## LET'S START WITH YOU NOVICES

What should you look for? The most important thing, which few people look into ahead of time, is an English-speaking ski school. Even in France, where English is

Here's an idea for you... **Look for key statistics. Calculate the vertical drop and the longest run and you can work out whether you'll be riding more lifts than you will pistes. Look at the number of lifts (especially high-speed ones if you want to maximise your time) and proportion of green, blue, red and black runs. Is there enough to keep you busy for the duration of your trip? If not, are there other resorts close by?**

commonly spoken in resorts, it's worth checking that there is a snowsports teacher who speaks fluent English. It's vital you understand instructions fully when learning.

It's also worth investigating ski and snowboard school techniques. Some resorts offer Burton's innovative Learn to Ride snowboard school, using specially designed boards that are easier to learn on. Many ski schools offer special beginner equipment, too. Ski Evolutif in Les Arcs, France, starts beginners off on skis as short as 100cm, and progress you to longer ones as your technique improves. The idea is that you learn to ski parallel on day one, so that by day six you're a confident intermediate.

Next on the list is a good selection of green and blue runs. Most brochures tell you this as a percentage of the total number of slopes. If it's your first ever week on snow, don't get too hung up about this. You won't need masses of piste choices because the chances are you'll stick to just one or two slopes. If you can look at the resort ski map ahead of time, see if there is a nice, long, green run so you won't be wasting time grappling with lifts.

## ONWARDS AND DOWNWARDS

Once you progress to intermediate, your choices expand even further. If you're going for more than a week, be sure to look at the total terrain and scan the piste map (try searching online for it). Is there enough to keep you entertained, on different slopes every day, for the duration of your stay?

Sölden in Austria certainly has enough to keep a confident intermediate happy for a week or more. It has wonderful wide runs that are great for confidence-boosting cruising. There's also plenty of accessible off-piste right next to, and in between, runs for those who want to get a taste of it. If you're off for a longer spell, try Vail in Colorado, which will entertain for weeks with its large proportion of red runs and five linked back bowls which are home to some easy blacks. There is also a great beginner terrain park with mini kickers and rails at neighbouring Beaver Creek.

Other good improvers' destinations that have miles of long, cruisy runs include Lake Tahoe in the Sierra Nevada (with enough ski areas dotted around the lake to keep you busy for months), Canada's Whistler (which works at any level) and Mayrhofen in Austria.

## IF IT'S STEEP AND DEEP YOU'RE AFTER

You'll find it in spades at Jackson Hole in the US (which has one of the world's scariest pisted drop-offs), extreme and freeride favourite Chamonix in France and Whistler/Blackcomb in Canada.

Val d'Isère in France is a great bet if you like your off-piste. As well as 300km of linked piste and 96 lifts, it also has some of the best lift-served off-piste in the world.

*Still confused? Pick one of the 'epic escapes' in Idea 36, Epic escapes, and you will find something for every level.*

*Try another idea…*

*'It is a great ability to be able to conceal one's ability.'*
FRANÇOIS DE LA ROCHEFOUCAULD's wise words don't apply to picking a pukka resort, though.

*Defining idea…*

179

Snowboarders often search for a different kind of terrain to skiers, with plenty of bowls, natural chutes and curving banks. Stellar boarding destinations include Fernie in Canada, Riksgransen in Sweden and Ste Foy in France.

*How did it go?*

**Q** **We're just as interested in the après as the ski. Can you recommend some great party ski towns?**

A   *No towns do nightlife quite as well as ski towns. In Austria, the world-class resort of St Anton and the British favourite, Mayrhofen, stand out. In both resorts, the après-ski scene starts to warm up at lunchtime. In St Anton, the final descent leaves from the Krazy Kanguruh bar, which has a permanent party atmosphere. In town you can take your pick from Europop bars and nightclubs to posh wine bars. Mayrhofen buzzes after hours too, with English, Irish and Scottish pubs, Euro bars and vast nightclubs. The Ice Bar, at the base of the main gondola, is reportedly Europe's biggest single sales point for Grolsch beer.*

**Q** **Can you recommend some good beginner resorts in Europe?**

A   *You're spoilt for choice in the Alps, but a few destinations do stand out. In France, La Plagne, a complex of 11 villages, is another great choice for beginners, with the easiest pistes to be found at Plagne Centre and Bellecôte. If you'd rather go somewhere small and friendly, try Les Contamines, a resort with plenty of confidence-building runs. Meanwhile at bigger brother Niederau in Austria is a lovely little Tyrolean resort that is ideal for beginners, with nursery slopes immediately behind the village centre. As you progress, you take a chair-lift up to a choice of drag-lifts and some wide, easy runs.*

# 42

# Child on board

**You're taking the family? A bit of preparation and the right questions are essential. Look for the best family-friendly facilities, top tips and the right time to get the kids on skis.**

The ski brochure shows a happy family shussing down the slopes together. What it doesn't show is harassed Mum trying to coax her tearful daughter down, and Dad sweet-talking the credit card company before forking out for childcare.

Yes, family skiing is always a challenge, but when you get it right the rewards are high.

I always swore that when I have kids, they'll be strapped to a snowboard by their second birthday. So imagine my (hypothetical) disappointment on discovering that it's bad for their postural development to get small fry on boards before about six or seven.

Here's an idea for you... **If you can afford to, it's always worth booking slopeside accommodation if you have a family. Being able to walk to the childcare facilities, the ski rental shop and to head back for a cheaper lunch in your apartment or hotel room, make any extra expense worthwhile.**

## HOW AND WHEN

The good news is, you can strap them to two planks without too many worries from toddling age, although ski schools traditionally start children at the age of four. If you do decide to strap the planks on as soon as they can walk, limit it to very short photo opportunity spells.

Resist the urge to teach your own offspring to ski (unless you want daily tantrums) and source a good ski school instead. For a number of years tour operators have been hiring their own English-speaking nannies and running well-equipped, well-organised crèches in many European and US resorts. But, when your kids get a bit older and you enrol them in ski school, especially where there is a language barrier, it can be more difficult.

Start by researching well ahead of time. Ski schools can get very booked up, especially during school holidays. Key questions to ask are what the instructor to child ratio is (you don't really want groups of more than six per class) and whether the instructors speak English.

Once booked, prepare your child by showing them pictures of you skiing or snowboarding and getting them to share your enthusiasm. Don't show them if you look at all nervous, because they are likely to pick this up in an instant. Try and strap them into their skis before they actually get there, even if it's just on the carpet the night before, as this will get them excited and familiar with the equipment.

## SOME TOP TIPS FOR FAMILIES

If, after a few lessons, you want to take your child up the hill yourself, don't ski behind them, holding them under the arms and sandwiched between your legs. This will only teach them to sit back and fall into your arms at the first sign of trouble. Instead, encourage independent balance and snow-plough beside them, giving them the handle of your ski pole to hold if necessary.

But you don't have to wait until your kids hit ski school age before you squeeze ski trips in – that would mean a serious hiatus from the hill for snow junkie parents.

Ski resorts have come along way in terms of childcare and many now have custom-built facilities, licensed trained staff and themed daily programmes. Still, it can be tough to leave your baby with unfamiliar people, even on the perfect powder day. To calm your fears, put in the research first.

Ask around to see if friends can recommend family-friendly resorts to head for (or steer clear of!), then follow up by looking at the resort website. If there is a dedicated kids' section, it's a good sign.

Always book and fill in registration times before you arrive in resort, and ask about the schedule and what is included. It's also a good idea to bring a list of your child's likes and dislikes, nap times and favourite toys. And be sure to ask where they post emergency messages and how they can be reached when you are on the slopes. Some resorts have

**Teach your kids the ski eco code outlined in Idea 50, *Tree hugging*, and help them respect the mountains.**

*Try another idea...*

**'Bringing up a family should be an adventure, not an anxious discipline in which everybody is constantly graded for performance.'**
MILTON R. SAPERSTEIN

*Defining idea...*

183

in-house extensions you can dial from on mountain phones, and a few progressive resorts have pagers for the parents to carry.

Finally, be there to pick your child up on time. It may be a bluebird powder day, but most resorts charge expensive late fees.

*How did it go?*

**Q**　**We want an easy destination where everything is on the door-step and we can dine out with our kids too.**

*A*　*Some of the world's most child-friendly resorts can be found in Scandinavia, with excellent, English-speaking childcare, doorstep skiing nursery slopes, family-friendly bars and restaurants. They also tend to have more than skiing on offer so you can go husky sledding, reindeer sleigh riding or ice skating too. Try Geilo in Norway, or a bigger resort like Åre in Sweden if you want enough terrain to challenge the adults too.*

**Q**　**We had real problems with the language barrier in French ski school. Can you recommend an English-speaking family friendly destination?**

*A*　*Breckenridge lives by the maxim 'a resort for which little folks are a big deal' and invests large amounts in its childcare facilities. As well as a decent ski area (240km) and a good snow record, it also has a Children's Centre baby nursery, one place at the Ski Kindergarten for three to five-year-olds and a Children's Ski & Ride School that offers written feedback and progress reports at the end of the day. The kindergarten runs a messaging system, with each parent issued with a pager in case of emergency.*

## 43

# Girls just wanna have fun

**Women learn faster when there are no guys around. No wonder women-specific ski and snowboard camps and clinics are becoming big business.**

The label 'women-only' doesn't mean a snowsports clinic for lightweights. Today you can find same-sex clinics for every ability. The benefits? More support, more self-confidence and less testosterone!

About half the resorts in the world now offer women-specific ski and snowboard programmes – that's how popular they've become. From novice clinics to gnarly camps, female-focused teaching has exploded.

### LET'S BE CLEAR, THIS IS NOT ABOUT MALE BASHING

There are real differences between the way men and women approach learning, especially when risk is involved. Girl-specific courses aim to use those differences to a woman's advantage.

Here's an idea for you...

**Feeling the fear? Women seem to experience fear more often and more intensely than men. Don't let inappropriate fear paralyse you. Instead, when you feel scared, take five long, deep breaths and repeat to yourself all the reasons why your fear is irrational (for example, the snow is soft and won't hurt, you know how to stop and so on).**

In the last decade, women's snowsports have been revolutionised by the advent of women-specific gear. For years, girls had to settle for equipment made for men that didn't take our physical differences into account.

Today we understand that physiological differences play a huge role. The 'Q' angle (the angle from our hips to our knees), centre of mass, bone length, foot shape, weight and strength are all different in men and women. All of these factors affect performance on the snow.

Now that manufacturers have run away with the women-specific boom, the girls are back on a more level playing field physically. Women-specific teaching aims to put them on a level playing field psychologically, too.

So why would you abandon your partner to play with the boys while you bond with the girls?

Well, there are many benefits to the single-sex environment. Women are typically less self-conscious when men aren't around. They worry less about making fools of themselves, they are less intimidated to try new things and they are less afraid to fail. Let's face it, boys can be competitive and, if you aren't comfortable with the added pressure of competition, it will sap your confidence. With these obstacles removed, you can focus all your energy on learning and improving.

Women are also thought to favour a different style of learning. Whereas men usually prefer to just get started and figure it out for themselves, women tend to prefer more detailed instruction, support and encouragement.

'Girls tend to be much more relaxed without guys around,' says Elissa Koskinen at Girlie Camps, one of the pioneers of women-specific winter camps across Europe. 'They can progress at their own tempo, without feeling intimidated, and take it easy until they are 100% sure. Girls are also really supportive of each other and push each other in a way guys never would. Guys push each other on a different level and much harder.'

It's also about support and camaraderie. Girls tend to thrive in a supportive environment and are more likely to offer support than men. They are also motivated by other women's achievements. 'When the girls see another girl doing a trick, they think "Wow, if she can do it, why not me?",' says Elissa. 'If a guy did the same trick, the girls would just think "Ah, that was a guy, I'll never be able to do anything like that anyway".' When women are surrounded by other women, intimidation gives way to support and encouragement, making it easier to easier to confront self-doubt and fear. And fear is a big issue for most of us.

Girls tend to be more scared of hurting themselves (even though it is said women have higher pain thresholds than men) and so feel more cautious. This is where women-specific teaching comes into its own, as instructors focus on working with their clients' fear, rather than trying to convince them there is no reason to worry. Female-focused teaching builds confidence slowly, rather than urging you to throw yourself over the edge.

**Got an attack of the wobbles? Turn to Idea 21, *Nailing nerves*, and find ways to fight your fear.**

*Try another idea…*

**'Courage, sacrifice, determination, commitment, toughness, heart, talent, guts. That's what little girls are made of; to hell with sugar and spice.'**

*Defining idea…*

Anon

187

*How did it go?*

**Q**  **I don't know where to start. Can you recommend some of the best women's ski and snowboard camps?**

*A*  *There are scores of girls-only camps world-wide now – a good web search will reveal hundreds of contacts for you to investigate. For snowboarding in Europe, Girlie Camps has one of the strongest reputations and runs year-round camps at classic resorts with pro riders brought in to inspire and teach. Women's-only winter sports programmes were born and bred in North America and there are dozens to choose from. Surf to www. skilikeawoman.com, an online directory of ski and snowboard lessons and programmes for women at more than 250 resorts world-wide.*

**Q**  **My boyfriend wants me to save the cash and teach me himself – good idea?**

*A*  *No! You may save your money, but you probably won't save your relationship. Learning to ski or snowboard can be a deeply personal and frustrating experience and all sorts of emotions are liable to get vented. If you get frustrated with yourself, at least in an objective, neutral and supportive teaching environment, you can pick yourself up and rationalise. If you're struggling in front of your man, you're more liable to feel defensive, he may feel impatient and the end result can be you taking it out on each other.*

# 44

# Party on the slopes

**What could be better than world-class skiing and snowboarding by day and A-list partying by night? There's a whole calendar of snowsports events that you cannot afford to miss.**

The ski season heralds a non-stop season of partying in the world of snowsports. Get out your diary and start planning with our guide to the most sought-after fun-fests in the snow.

No one does partying quite like skiers and snowboarders. No wonder so many resorts are known more for their après-ski than their ski. Most of them do it so well.

But there are literally hundreds of events in the snowsports calendar that sound like amazing, must-attend events. If you want to squeeze in some world-class sliding, amid world-class athletes, alongside some world-class partying, which ones should you highlight in the diary?

## THE CANDIDE THOVEX INVITATIONAL

*What it is.* Candide Thovex, leader of the freestyle ski movement and three times winner of the X-Games, invites the most talented freestylers of the moment for two days of riding in his home town of La Clusaz.

*By day.* Jaw-dropping freestyle moves from more than 100 top riders in a relaxed jam-style session, far from the pressure of competitions, judging and ranking amid the steep slopes of the Balme massif.

*By night.* Chilled-out fun and reggae beats in a Jamaican atmosphere after-party with more than 1,600 people.

## VERBIER RIDE

*What it is.* The grandest manifestation of freeriding in the world with a strong international reputation, the Ride series manages to preserve the big mountain freeriding spirit.

*By day.* Big mountain riding from the 3023m summit of Verbier's famous Mont Gelé, where the freeskiers choose their line and express their own style down the west face, dropping cliffs, cornices and skiing technically difficult but controlled lines. SkierCross and Slope Style competitions also draw the crowds.

*By night.* A festival atmosphere pervades the town. Head for the Farinet, Casbah, Pub Mont Fort, Wonderbar and Tara Tata after hours.

*Here's an idea for you…* **Need a new ride? Test out the latest skis and snowboards, and experience one of Europe's best après-ski parties at the Mondial du Ski in the lively resort of Les Deux Alpes in France.**

## THE WORLD SKI & SNOWBOARD FESTIVAL, WHISTLER, CANADA

*What it is.* North America's largest snowsports and music event and a showcase for some of the greatest riding on earth.

*By day.* The world's best (strictly invitees only) battle it out in every on-hill discipline. Breathtaking.

*By night.* For 10 nights Whistler reverberates with electricity generated by legendary music, outdoor concerts and film showings. Combine this with Whistler's youthful party atmosphere, and you've got some wild nights on your hands.

## SNOWBOMBING

*What it is .* Boarding by day, beats by night, this is a European Woodstock in the snow and definitely more about the party than the sport.

*By day.* With the night-time events pushing on until dawn, you'll probably do more sleeping than skiing or riding. But you can always watch the freestyle pros taking part in jam sessions and risking life and limb doing breathtaking stunts.

*By night.* Seven days of pure hedonism with 50 top DJs and 20 live bands.

**With all this partying you're going to need to prepare your liver first. Turn to Idea 10, *Après-ski angels*, and find out how to pretox before the party season.**

Try another idea...

## THE ARCTIC CHALLENGE

*What it is.* The Arctic Challenge is a snowboarding event created by world champion Terje Haakonsen. It is considered the ultimate snowboarding event.

*By day.* Held in the far north of Norway, the best boarders in the world gather to compete in disciplines such as 'highest air' and 'best trick'.

*By night.* Lots of drinking, lots of partying in a friendly atmosphere.

## THE BRITS

*What it is.* The British Freestyle Ski and Snowboard Championships is *the* event of the year for riders on the thriving UK scene. This week-long competition is open to anyone, from professional riders to amateurs with attitude, making for an eclectic mix of styles, abilities and personalities.

*By day.* Plenty of 'oohs' and 'aahs' as you watch Britain's best catch some serious air in the half-pipe, the boarder-cross, slopestyle and big air events, and plenty of giggles listening to the funniest MCs around.

*Defining idea...*

**'One just has to watch, to listen, and to be moved by the moment. The performances command our humility and respect.'**
STEVE KLASSEN, the freeride legend and five times winner of the Verbier Xtreme.

*By night.* This is resort atmosphere at its finest – the vibe is small, friendly and fun. You'll mingle with Britain's best riders and dance to celebrity DJs.

**Q**  **I get enough of skiing and snowboarding on the slopes during the day – are there any big spectator events that include other winter sports?**

*How did it go?*

**A**  *Try the Winter X Games, usually held in Colorado. A broader winter action sports event, the X Games feature amazing athletes from across the globe competing for medals in snowmobiling and moto-cross, as well as skiing and snowboarding. Here the contests continue into the night, so you can get your own sliding in during the day and soak up the festival atmosphere and death-defying tricks after hours.*

**Q**  **I'm inspired. Any chance I can enter any of these contests next year?**

**A**  *A lot of the biggest events on the snowsports calendar are by invitaion only (for contestants, not spectators). But there a few notable exceptions. The main 'free for all' competition for skiers is the Verbier Ride. All three disciplines are open to accomplished, aspiring skiers that are eager to compete with the pros and sponsored riders. And if you have, or can blag, a British passport, The Brits welcomes aspiring amateurs, both skiers and snowboarders.*

# 45

# Endless winter

**What do you do when the snow melts? Chase it around the globe, find a glacier, get to grips with dry slopes ... who says snowsports are seasonal?**

There is something satisfying about fooling Mother Nature by squeezing in some sneaky snow time in summer. And, with more than 200 places where you can slide on snow between June and September, you don't have to wait until next season.

I can't remember the last time I had a summer beach holiday. In fact, for the last decade, I've done my damnedest to avoid summer altogether by chasing winter around the globe.

But a summer ski trip doesn't necessarily mean forking out for a round the world ticket to ride the Kiwi cruisers. Some of the best summer snowsports can be found right on your doorstep.

## LET'S START WITH DRY SLOPES

Stop groaning. If the last time you tried it was learning to snowplough before that school trip to the mountains, it's time to give it another chance. Surfaces have improved dramatically and you can now cruise on artificial snow in vast indoor domes.

*Here's an idea for you...* **Don't bother booking accommodation before you go summer skiing in the northern hemisphere. This is off-peak time in the mountains and you can get some great deals just by turning up and hunting around for the best.**

Such is their popularity, there are now almost four dozen worldwide. The UK is at the forefront of dry slope skiing but other European countries, especially Germany, are also embracing dry riding. The US is slower on the uptake, but a few slopes are now available there.

If you're not lucky enough to live near a 'real snow' indoor slope, you'll probably be stuck with Dendix, a matting material devised in the 1960s, and made up of small brushes. It's a far cry from the more modern stuff but is still handy when it comes to learning the basics and brushing up your skills in the summer.

## FURTHER AFIELD

If you're willing to travel, consider glacier skiing. The slopes are quiet, the temperature is warm and, once you get down the mountain after lunch, you can still make the most of the incredible array of summer sports mountain resorts have to offer.

In Europe, there are four glacier resorts that stand out above all others – Les Deux Alpes and Tignes in France, Sölden in Austria, Zermatt in Switzerland. And there are plenty of smaller glaciers in the Alps and in the Austrian Tyrol if you fancy making a bit of a summer tour – seek and ye shall find.

Another snow sure-summer option is to head north up to the Arctic Circle where the season stretches well into July. Iceland and Riks-gränsen, in northern Sweden, are the two great places to ski under the midnight sun.

In North America, summer snow seekers aren't so lucky – Whistler in Canada is the only resort that offers summer glacier skiing, but California's Mammoth Mountain and Oregon's Timberline on Mount Hood have winter seasons that last well into summer anyway.

But if it's deep powder snow you're hunting, you really will have to work for it as the southern hemisphere hides all summer stashes. New Zealand's Southern Alps are among the best. Snowboarders and good skiers will love the terrain at Treble Cone, while beginners will prefer the shorter slopes at Coronet Peak and The Remarkables.

South America is also booming in popularity as a summer snowsports destination and, as resorts grow and improve, they are finally approaching world-class level.

The snow can be world-class too. In Chilean resorts like Portillo and Valle Nevado, storms and clearing high-pressure systems are large and powerful, producing periods of heavy

**Now you've been training all summer, head for a truly world-class destination next winter. Turn to Idea 36, *Epic escapes*, and pick an all-time classic.**

*Try another idea…*

*'Sunshine is delicious, rain is refreshing, wind braces us up, snow is exhilarating; there is really no such thing as bad weather, only different kinds of good weather.'*
JOHN RUSKIN knew how to look on the bright side whether it's summer or winter.

*Defining idea…*

197

snow followed by perfectly blue skies. Single storms have dumped as much as 30ft of snow on the central Andes.

In Argentina, those who want to be challenged should head for Les Lenas between June and October. There are no flats so you can ski 3,000ft of consistent stuff, often in great snow.

*How did it go?*

**Q** **I want to head down under to ski New Zealand. Is there a pass I can get that's valid at all ski resorts, or do I have to buy a new one each time?**

*A* *Unfortunately there isn't a pass that's valid for the whole of New Zealand, but several ski areas have got together to make your tourist dollar go further. Treble Cone and Cardrona have a minor team-up for 'Tourist Week' passes and www.NZSki.com offers a combined pass for their resorts of The Remarkables, Coronet Peak and Mount Hutt, which also includes Ohau. There's also a 'Chill Pass' that gives access to all the club fields around Arthur's Pass.*

**Q** **Does summer skiing mean summer temperatures? Will I need shorts and T-shirt or snow pants and goggles?**

*A* *All the usual rules of the mountain apply, which means you need to be prepared for anything. Weather in the mountains can change quickly and I've been on glaciers in the middle of July in near-blizzard conditions. But, on the whole, you are likely to get warmer temperatures, so it will pay to take a sunscreen with a high SPF, a lightweight snowsports jacket and sunglasses.*

## 46

# Avalanche!

**Off-piste riding may be the ultimate adrenalin rush, but if you aren't avalanche aware, it could also be the last rush you ever experience. Wise up to where it's safe to slide.**

Avalanches do not 'just happen'. These terrifying slides happen for specific reasons in specific conditions. The more you understand about avalanches and their causes, the better you will be able to avoid risky situations.

### KNOWLEDGE IS SAFETY

There are few things more terrifying than the 'white death'. If you've ever been on-piste and heard the distant rumble of avalanche as the mountain patrol team carries out controlled explosions, you'll have some idea of their awesome power.

Skiing and boarding, especially off-piste, can be a risky business. Every year avalanches kill, but most victims are not taken by huge, crushing waves of snow. More often (in about 75% of incidents) they are victims of smaller wind slab avalanches.

Here's an idea for you...

**Not sure if that slope is safe? Classic danger signs are: steep, open, convex slopes; large dumps of new snow (over 20cm); wind-blown snow and high winds, especially overnight and controlled explosions being done on nearby pistes. South-facing slopes on hot days in spring are the most dangerous places a freerider could be. If in doubt, don't go there.**

As the name suggests, the most common cause is wind. It carries snow over ridges and drops it on sheltered lee slopes, building a thick, unstable layer of dense snow. If the layers of snow don't stick strongly, the slab will slide given the slightest disturbance.

Wind slab avalanches are most likely to happen on slopes between 28° and 45°, the perfect incline for skiing and boarding. And because the instability can be hidden under a layer of inviting powder, they can be hard to predict.

Powder avalanches are less common and are the ones you've probably seen on TV documentaries and in films. They can level buildings and destroy anything in their path. Powder slides happen after a heavy snowfall on steep slopes over 45°. As a slide starts, it will pick up more and more snow on the way and reach speeds of 250mph. Although rare, especially in Europe, this type of avalanche is extremely dangerous, battering or choking its victims to death.

The third type of avalanche is a wet snow avalanche, which happen during periods of warm weather, usually on south-facing slopes. As water drains from the melting surface snow, it can permeate through the snow pack to a weak layer. As the layer becomes saturated it gets heavier until it falls. Your chances of surviving a wet snow avalanche are practically nil as once they stop, they set like concrete and buried victims are unable to move or breathe.

So how can you tell how safe a slope is? Even though there is a science to it, predicting slides can be extremely difficult, because you don't know what's beneath the snow. A slope can be made unstable from weak layers many metres under the surface.

Turn to Idea 33, *Piste off*, for other off-piste essentials.

*Try another idea...*

The most thorough method of checking involves digging a hole in a similar slope to check if the layers of snow are stable. To learn how to do this, take a course in snow safety. Even if you have done a backcountry course, take a guide with you off-piste. Guides know the local area, the local weather and will be in constant contact with patrollers.

## AN ESSENTIAL ITEM

If you are buried in an avalanche for more than 15 minutes, your chance of survival drops by 50%. Every second is crucial, so wearing an avalanche transceiver is vital.

A transceiver is a radio device with two modes, 'transmit' and 'receive'. Switch it to 'transmit' when you ride. If one of your group is buried by an avalanche, you and your remaining friends should turn each unit to 'receive' mode to locate the buried person. Do this before you try to go for help. The signal will get louder as you get closer.

If you have programmed the emergency services and mountain rescue into your mobile phone, call for help. But be aware that mobile phones may interfere with some transceivers, so it's best to leave them switched off while you're actually riding.

*'I want to stay as close to the edge as I can without going over. Out on the edge you see all kinds of things you can't see from the centre.'*
KURT VONNEGUT

*Defining idea...*

*How did it go?*

**Q**   **There are a few tracks where I want to ride. Surely that means it's pretty safe, especially on skis?**

A   *OK, time to bust a few myths. Tracks in the snow do not mean a slope is safe. The conditions may have changed and the riders who went before you may just have got lucky. Don't assume that because someone else has been there, it's safe for you. Secondly, you're no safer just because you're on skis. Snowboarders are not more likely to cause avalanches than skiers. In fact, when you're riding on weak layers of snow, skiers actually add more stress to the snow pack than boarders.*

   *Oh, and why do you say 'I'? You should never freeride alone. Only venture off-piste in groups of three or more, otherwise if you get into trouble, you're on your own.*

**Q**   **What should I do if I'm caught in an avalanche?**

A   *Luck plays the greatest role, but there a few things that experts reckon may boost your chances of survival. As soon as you see the slide, try to ride out, by escaping to the side if you can, or by out-gunning the avalanche. If neither looks possible, throw off your skis, poles and rucksack and try to unstrap your snowboard so that you can 'swim' towards the surface. If you're near big trees or solid rocks, grab hold of something.*

   *If the snow and debris catch you up, curl up and protect your mouth and nose with your hands and start to dig a breathing space as soon as the slide stops.*

## 47

# Hill highway code

**You've mastered the ski hill, the slopes are yours and you feel like king of the mountain. Reality check: you have to share these slopes with an ever-burgeoning band of other snowsports junkies. Be kind to your fellow skier and learn the ski code.**

Unfortunately you can't have the pistes to yourself all the time, but you can make them safer, thanks to a new international highway code for the hill.

Ski in the States and you'll immediately want to make sure you're aware of the ski and snowboard code of conduct. The threat of legal action against the resorts, individuals and those who don't follow 'the rules' seems to get greater every year and if you're in an accident, you'll want to be sure you were sticking to the code.

Even if you're riding in Europe or the southern hemisphere, it pays to follow the rules of the mountain for your own safety as well as that of others. The FIS (International Ski Federation) recently established 10 rules for the conduct of skiers and snowboarders. They exist for your safety, so gen up and follow them at all times.

*Here's an idea for you…* **Consider taking a qualified mountain guide (IFMGA). They may cost a bit more, but their knowledge and expertise could save your life. If they've got the risk dialled, all you have to worry about is not boring your audience with tales of your epic day in the bar later.**

1  *Respect*: Do not endanger others. Kamikaze speed races may be fun for you and your mates, but they're not for the wobbly novice halfway down.

2  *Control*: Adapt the manner and speed of your skiing to your ability and to the general conditions on the mountain. In other words, don't hurl yourself off a black run just because your mates have.

3  *Choice of route*: The skier or snowboarder in front has priority – leave enough space. This isn't the place to tailgate.

4  *Overtaking*: Leave plenty of space when overtaking a slower skier or snowboarder. Remember how shaken it left you as a novice when good riders whizzed past at close quarters?

5  *Entering and starting*: Look up and down the mountain each time before starting or entering a marked run. Those on the piste already have right of way. Just because you're faster, it doesn't mean you can cut in.

6  *Stopping*: Only stop at the edge of the piste or where you can easily be seen. Snowboarders who park in packs like meerkats in the middle, take note!

7  *Climbing*: When climbing up or down, always keep to the side of the piste.

8  *Signs*: Obey all signs and markings – they are there for your safety. Ignore them and you could be signing your own death certificate.

9  *Assistance*: In case of accidents provide help and alert the rescue service. Let the St Bernard in you prevail.

10  *Identification*: All those involved in an accident, including witnesses, should exchange names and addresses. Don't disappear because it's easier; someone may need your help.

But it's not just on the piste that you need to stick to the rules. Recent advances in ski and snowboard technology mean more riders than ever are heading into the backcountry. Even virtual beginners can now experience the buzz of freeriding, and although they may be able to manage the whole mountain, they don't necessarily manage the safety aspect. That buzz doesn't come without risk, so follow some basic rules to make sure you and your posse stay alive.

First, never venture off-piste with fewer than three riders. If one person gets injured there is somebody with them while the other goes for help. If you want to ride en masse, be aware that a larger group will place more stress on the snowpack. When you get out there, never traverse the slope above others. You could trigger a slide that would bury your friends and possibly yourself.

At the very least, always check the weather forecast and the area you plan to ride. Getting stranded can mean a long journey home. Talk to the local ski patrol before you head out. If you're lucky, they may give you the low-down on the area you plan to ride, advice on where the best powder is and where is unsafe.

If it's warm, set your alarm and leave first thing in the morning. Changing temperatures are the cause of many natural avalanches, especially on powder days. Most avalanches happen on slopes between 28° and 45°, so try to assess where you ride.

**Heading off-piste? If you want to freeride in safety, bone up on your off-piste awareness in Idea 33, *Piste off*.**

*Try another idea…*

**'Take calculated risks. That is quite different from being rash.'**

GEORGE S. PATTON

*Defining idea…*

205

*How did it go?*

**Q    My mates and I are ready to try some off-piste en masse. What should we be aware of?**

A    *Firstly, try not to go 'en masse'. The weight of multiple riders at any one time can cause instability on the snow, which is dangerous not only to your group, but to others around you. Instead, go out in small groups. If in doubt, ride a slope one at a time to a safer place, such as behind a big rock.*
      *Secondly, make sure you have some avalanche awareness. Either enrol on a course or take a guide.*

**Q    I frequently get tired on my way down the piste. Is it OK to keep sitting down and resting?**

A    *Yes, rest whenever you feel the need, but do it at the side of the piste so that you aren't blocking the way for other piste users. Be careful not to stop just over the brow of a hill – you will be hidden from view to anyone descending. And make sure you have a companion who is happy to stop with you. If you tire easily, it's never a good idea to ride alone.*

# 48

# Become a man or woman magnet

**Training to be a ski or snowboard instructor needn't take years. Nowadays you can earn your wings faster. Sabbatical anyone?**

If you're hooked on the mountains, the snowsports and the Great Outdoors, spending every day on the slopes must be the ultimate job. But getting trained properly takes planning and care, so follow our guide and turn your passion into a profession.

### 'I'M A SNOWSPORTS INSTRUCTOR'

Mmm, sounds good doesn't it? I've thought about it, all my friends who love the mountains have considered it; in fact, anyone who loves snowsports and mountain living has probably mulled it over at some point.

Here's an idea for you... **Look for a course that has a broad training programme. If you can, opt for one that is more a mountain education than just straight instructor lessons. A good course syllabus will include technical training, avalanche awareness, first aid, team leading, freestyle, sports science and sports psychology.**

And why not? There are some fantastic perks of the job. Firstly, and the real reason you'll do it, you get to spend every day out on the slopes. Secondly, you'll get a free lift pass; and finally, you'll get major respect in the resort.

But the truth is, being a snowsports instructor is tough. It's mentally and physically demanding, the clients can be difficult, the hours long and the training expensive.

Still not put off? Right, let's give you the lowdown.

How good do you need to be to train as a snowsports instructor? Not as expert as you might think. 'You should be able to make it down reds and blacks, not necessarily with great style, but at least have the ability to control your descent,' says Warren Smith at Warren Smith Ski Academy. 'Remember for your first level the aim is to make you into a ski instructor, not expect you to be one when you turn up.'

Teaching snowsports is a very passionate job, but it is also demanding. To succeed you need to *want* to teach because of your love and appreciation of the mountains, because you want to help others share your passion and because you want to become a better rider. Technical knowledge is important, but good communication and the ability to establish relationships are the most valuable skills.

Once you've decided you're up to it, the next step is to find a course and get your wings. Ski certification is a tricky business. Each country demands official accreditation, and qualifications from one country may not necessarily allow you to teach in another. So getting yourself lined up for the right one is vital.

**Tap into the sports psychology in Idea 35, *Winning the mind game*, and instil some confidence in your troops.**

*Try another idea...*

## DO YOUR RESEARCH FIRST

Decide where you want to work and check out the qualification requirements before you sign up for a course. For example, some resorts in France demand extra skills, while the PSIA (Professional Ski Instructors of America) basic level is not considered advanced enough to find a teaching job in France or New Zealand.

The most respected qualifications are top-level ones. But top level differs across the world. If you do a BASI (British Association of Snowsport Instructors) course, the top level is level one. This is the one that allows you to open your own ski school and train other ski instructors. Across the rest the world, every country has an international top level called level three.

Your best bet is to look at courses that lead to qualifications recognised by the International

*'There is probably no profession in the entire world more Zen than ski instruction. For ski instructors, each day dawns with fresh opportunities to discover something new about themselves, their students, and the awe-inspiring mountains in which they work.'*

PETER KRAY

*Defining idea...*

209

Ski Instructors Association (www.isiaski.org), the umbrella organisation for snowsport instructors.

Once you've found the right qualification, find the right course. Ask what level of qualification the ski coach who is hosting the course holds. It should be international (level one in the UK and level three in the rest of the world).

Next, ensure that the price you are quoted is an 'all-in' fee. It should at least include training and examination fees, first aid certification and lift pass. A good training course will also have an agreement with a ski and snowboard school that enables you to get a job placement during and after the course

Lastly, make sure the company is reputable, with a history you can research. Ask for references from past pupils and ask a few ski schools in the area you want to work if they have heard of them.

**Q** **Who should I contact to find out which qualification is valid in each different country?**

*How did it go?*

**A** *Your best bet is to contact the snowsports instructors association in the country you're looking to work in. They will tell you exactly what the requirements are and where they recommend to train.*

*Contact the International Ski Instructors' Association (+41 31 810 41 11), known better by the acronym ISIA, which is the world body for professional instructors. It has 36 member nations and will put you in touch with the right association in your chosen country.*

**Q** **I'm qualified! Any advice to help me become an even better instructor?**

**A** *Treat your clients as individuals. Knowing or being aware of why someone skis or snowboards is the best way to understand his or her personal experience on snow, and the quickest way to discover not only what, but how this person learns. For people to take that little risk you need them to, they have to trust you and know that you've been listening to them.*

*Some people learn by listening. Some learn by watching. Some learn by doing. By asking questions, listening to the answers, and watching a student's response, a good instructor can see how they can help best. Oh, and take time to stop to smell the roses now and again. Don't forget why you're here.*

## 49

# Sex and the chalet

**Want to stay on the slopes all winter? Whether you opt to pull pints, serve in a chalet or help out on the chair-lift, doing a season well takes planning.**

The pay-offs for working a season in a ski resort are huge — the skiing, the snow and of course, the nightlife. The pay, however, is anything but. Still up for it? Here's what you need to know.

Oh, how I used to envy those chalet girls who got to stay on in the snow when I had to go home to the rain. All I saw was their hedonistic lives of sun, sex and snow. Having heard the tales of many a seasonaire, I now know that, yes, that's part of it, but it's far from the whole picture. If you're expecting an easy life, you're in for a shock.

Once you realise you're going to have to work hard for your snow time, the first step in becoming a fully-fledged seasonaire is to find the right job. If you want the security of working for a big company and are anxious not to arrive in resort without a job, consider applying to be a tour rep. This is a demanding, but rewarding, job. The smooth running of your guests' holiday is in your hands. You'll

Here's an idea for you... **Trying to decide which resort to spend your season in? Think small. A bigger resort might sound like more fun, but you often get much more out of the short time you are there in a smaller community.**

be expected to solve guests' problems, run the transfers to and from resort (be warned, transfer days will be long and testing), liaising with ski shops, hotels and lift pass companies, lead après-ski events and reach set sales targets for lift passes and ski hire. If you're lucky, you may also be asked to do some ski guiding. The perks of the job are getting a free lift pass, free equipment hire and extra earnings from the après-ski and tips. The downside is that you'll be working hard for them, probably six or seven days a week.

Tour operators also employ chalet staff, which can be a great way to spend your season, and will often earn you good tips and even good friends if you get lucky with your guests.

Maximise your chances by knowing what tour operators are looking for. Look at the company's website or brochure before the interview, and go with an idea of which of their resorts you'd like to work in. If you are interviewed for a chalet position, make sure you know how to cook the meals on your menu plan.

The key requirement of these jobs is social skills. You'll be spending a large part of your day interacting with guests so make sure you come across as sparky, confident and friendly.

When I went for my interview with a tour operator, it was done with a group. This is very common, so go prepared with a few fascinating facts about yourself ready to dazzle the group with.

## GOT THE JOB?

Brace yourself for an overseas training course at least two weeks before the first guests arrive. Remember that just because you are on the training course, it doesn't mean you're out of the woods. If you don't come up to scratch you'll be packed off home. It may feel rough justice, but try to remember you're not on holiday.

**Want to work a season but would rather do it on the slopes? Turn to Idea 48, *Become a man or woman magnet*, and find out how to train as a snowsports instructor.**

*Try another idea...*

If you're happy to wait until you get to your chosen resort to look for work, go with a few prepared CVs, tailored to different types of resort job, such as waiting in a restaurant, serving in a bar, housekeeping in a hotel, or if you're a good skier or snowboarder, a ski guide. If you can highlight your skills that are most relevant to the job, you stand a better chance.

Many jobs will entitle you to at least a subsidised lift pass and, if you're lucky, you'll get live-in accommodation, but expect to have to share a room.

At the start of the season it can be tempting to ski all day and party all night. Try to pace yourself. Think how you feel after a one week ski trip when you're allowed lie in. If you have to get up early and work every day, you'll be heading for burnout.

You may be surprised at how little slope time you actually get. Give yourself chance to ease into a routine and try not to be disheartened if you can't find much ski time at first. When

*'Just because I slept with you it doesn't mean I have to ski with you.'*
A seasonaire's T-shirt slogan says it all.

*Defining idea...*

your day off does roll around (yes, you'll probably only get one), don't waste it by lying in with a hangover. This could be your only time to ride, and since that's why you came, get up there early!

*How did it go?*

**Q** **I've got a job organised – should I take my own ski or snow-board?**

A *If you're a snowboarder you may already have a customised board that you should take for street cred value. If you're a skier and have boots that fit, then definitely take them.  Skis are not so necessary. If you get on well with your local hire shop, you'll be able to try every type of ski, not worry (as much) about trashing the bases, get them serviced whenever you want and then buy the ones you like best at a discount at the end of the season.*

**Q** **Will my standard holiday insurance be enough to cover me all season?**

A *No. Standard holiday insurance usually covers you only for a specified number of ski days, not a whole season of skiing. Some specialist snowsports insurance companies have tailored packages for resort workers. Check your policy covers medical expenses, legal liability and personal accident. In France you can also buy a 'Carte Neige' with your lift pass that will cover you off-piste.*

# 50

# Tree hugging

**What's the point in learning to ski or board if global warming melts all the snow? From tree planting to learning the eco-code, snowsports are finally getting eco-friendly.**

Experts warn that in 50 years, recreational snowsports could be a thing of the past. As a consumer, there are things you can do to stop that from becoming the reality. Are you helping to protect and preserve?

Felling whole forests to create new pistes, erecting power-hungry lift systems and flying in visitors from all over the world. Mmm, skiing and snowboarding resorts aren't exactly known for their green credentials.

But that's all changing. New threats are emerging, illustrating the delicate state of mountain areas. Chief among them is global warming, which could even precipitate the end of ski-related tourism. Suddenly skiers and snowboarders are having to sit up and listen.

Here's an idea for you... **About to book your next trip to the slopes? Think about your contribution to CO$_2$ emissions. Yes, you need to get there somehow, but consider flying fewer miles or switching from air to rail.**

According to a report by the United Nations Environmental Program, half of all Alpine ski resorts in France, Austria and Switzerland may be forced to close over the next 50 years if current global warming trends continue, and the snowline rises another 300 metres to 1800 metres above sea level.

Unfortunately, many of the threatened resorts have reacted by desperately trying to colonise the remaining pristine peaks at the highest altitudes. Some have succeeded in getting permission to build so-called 'second generation ski resorts' above the revised snowline among the highest peaks and glaciers.

Even summer skiing is at risk as we lose our glaciers. Huge swathes of ice needed to support plant and animal life in the mountains have already disappeared, causing environmental hazards such as rock slides. The statistics are scary; glaciers shrank by an average of 18% between 1985 and 2000 (in the previous 130 years they shrank at a steady 2% per decade).

Nor is it just global warming you should be worried about. According to research published in the British Ecological Society's *Journal of Applied Ecology*, machine piste-bashing and artificial snow production is destroying delicate alpine plants too.

And, this damage is long-lasting. But as ski resorts begin to feel the heat of climate change, and use more artificial snow to keep us snow junkies happy, the risks to plant life increase.

It's not hard to see how heavy piste bashers damage vegetation as they flatten the runs, but artificial snow? This stuff tends to melt later than the real thing, and is made from river and lake water that contains more minerals and other chemical compounds than natural snow.

## BE AWARE AND INVOLVED

Worried? You should be. The good news is there is plenty you can do to help. Many of skiing and snowboarding's governing bodies have now issued their own codes of practice for the eco-aware winter sports athlete.

Begin by being more aware of your environmental impact: find out as much as you can. Build on this awareness by checking your own impact – don't litter the slopes, for example, and respect your natural habitat.

Choose a resort with environmentally friendly practices and encourage your operator to adopt green policies.

At home you can take this still further by recycling whenever you can and reducing energy use. Some winter tour operators are also getting in on the act, offering customers the chance to pay a small premium to make their trip carbon-neutral (trees planted with your money will soak up $CO_2$) and investing in renewable energy projects. Ask your chosen operator what it is doing – if nothing, vote with your feet. Every little really does help.

**With all this weird weather you'll need gear that can stand up to unpredictability. Turn to Idea 11, *Weather any white-out*, and discover the best fabrics and functions to look for.**

*Try another idea…*

*'Never believe that a few caring people can't change the world. For, indeed, that's all who ever have.'*
MARGARET MEAD (1901–1978)
anthropologist

*Defining idea…*

*How did it go?*

**Q** **I want to stay somewhere that embraces eco-initiatives. Where do you suggest?**

*A* *US resorts tend to be streets ahead of European ones in terms of embracing the whole environmental protection issue. Aspen in Colorado probably does more than any other resort to be seen as green. It has a director responsible for environmental affairs, produces regular sustainability reports and has won awards for its schemes to reduce the impact of skiing. It uses a micro-hydroelectric power plant, which uses the resort's existing snowmaking system to channel spring water run-off through a turbine, generating electricity, and uses biodiesel to drive its snowcats.*

*But the Alps has eco-heroes too. One of the most exciting is a futuristic-looking dome-shaped camp above Villars in the Swiss Alps called Whitepod that provides a tranquil winter setting while having a minimal impact on the environment.*

**Q** **Terrifying. Is it all doom and gloom, and will I really be throwing my skis away in a few years?**

*A* *There has been an avalanche of disastrous predictions for the future of snowsports, but don't throw your skis away just yet. Global warming is a controversial issue and some experts have also predicted a modification in the Gulf Stream as the Arctic ice melts. This could make the French Alps even colder and might make skiing on the English Downs a possibility! Getting the 'right' amount of snow in a season, it may only depend on just two or three big dumps on the right dates. In the next 10 to 20 years all the signs point to the trend for poor snow at low altitude, but with several real winters continuing. After that, you'll probably need money and time to reach the highest peaks ahead of everyone else.*

## 51

# Cutting edges

**Skiwear that communicates, base layers that monitor blood sugar and skis that turn for you. From fashion and freestyle to technology and gadgets, what's the future in snowsports?**

Gone are the days when all a ski jacket did was keep you warm. Nowadays, mountain wear is multitasking, interactive and super high-tech. Can you keep up?

I remember my first ever snowsports outfit. It was neon pink (such a great look in the 80s) and … er, actually that's about it. It was pink.

OK, so it kept me warm. Well, warmish. But that was all it did. Fast forward 20 years and my mountain gear keeps me warm, it breathes so that I stay dry, it helps me communicate thanks to in-built gadgets and, if I were to upgrade to the next model, it would even be able to recharge itself with solar panels.

Yes, if you've got the money and like to stay at the cutting edge of cool, skiing and snowboarding are the perfect sports in which to indulge your James Bond side. So where are we at with high-tech hedonism?

Here's an idea for you... **Want to stay at the cutting edge of cool? Be the first to hear of the snowsports trends on the horizon by getting in touch with ISPO (www.ispo.com); a global trade show that forecasts trends and showcases the next season's products way ahead of time.**

Well, jackets lead the way in wearable technology, with built-in radios, microphones, earpieces and 'push-to-talk' technology for hands-free communication. Even if an MP3 player isn't built-in, an MP3 pocket and understated portals for earphones have become a winter essential.

On the more practical side of high altitude style, jackets are now controlling how hot you feel and how well you can see. Powered by small battery packs, some jackets have electroluminescent panels that light up on low visibility days (or when you're stumbling back to the chalet after a few après-ski drinks). If the mulled wine doesn't warm you up, some manufacturers are now producing clothing with battery-driven heating, which warms you up at the push of a button. This technology is also available in mittens, and so cold hands are a thing of the past.

Futuristic fabrics such as soft shell mean skiwear doesn't have to be bulky to be effective. Soft, breathable and water-repellent, soft shell regulates body temperature but is lightweight and stretchy, allowing designers to create sleek, figure-hugging styles.

If you're not wearing your gadgets, there are plenty of high-tech options you can carry that will mark you out as a futuristic snow rider. Among the most useful for speed demons are watches that can measure and store both your maximum speed and average speed of a run. With altimeter, barometer, compass, stop watch and PC interface, wearing a watch like this means you can suss out your day's activity, record it and, most importantly, brag about it in the bar afterwards.

Other manufacturers have launched two-way adventure radios, designed to withstand a harsh environment and provide extra communication range (often up to five miles) – perfect if you're on their home turf and want to save on international mobile phone roaming costs.

But it's in the area of safety where advanced technology and new ideas are really proving their worth. Avalanche airbags have been developed to work as a backpack with an exploding double airbag stored in the side pockets, leaving enough room in the middle of the pack for your personal kit. If you are caught in an avalanche, the airbag will inflate and rise to the top of the debris and snow, indicating to rescuers exactly where you are.

**Now you know the technology of the future, turn to Idea 4, *Cheap thrills*, and find out how to save on your trip so that you can afford the gadgets.**

*Try another idea…*

*'Any sufficiently advanced technology is indistinguishable from magic.'*
ARTHUR C. CLARKE

*Defining idea…*

**Q** **With the onset of global warming threatening our ski hills, what's the future for indoor snowsports?**

A    *Indoor snow domes with artificial snow are cropping up at destinations across the world at a rate of knots. Even furnace-like Dubai now has a resort with tumbling snowflakes, skiing and snowboarding on five trails. But snow domes are already becoming passé. Next on the horizon are snow-covered treadmills. Yes, you heard right. This magnet-propelled indoor ski slope called Ski-Trac, dreamt up by an Aussie inventor, works by spinning a 50m wide, snow-covered disc tilted at an angle to create a sloped surface. As you ride down, the disc spins in the opposite direction beneath your skis or snowboard. Once you hit the bottom, you simply stop and ride the 'hill' back to the top.*

**Q** **What's the one futuristic snowsports gadget guaranteed to impress?**

A    *Helmets are no longer just functional safety devices, they have finally attained cool status. But none is cooler than a lid fitted with new interactive military technology from the Japanese company Olaf Li. This cool piece of kit fits to any helmet and offers the geographically-challenged 'head-up display' that tells you the time, temperature, your speed, direction of travel and height above sea level. Placed on the helmet and directly in your field of vision, it can also be hooked up with a GPS unit, displaying a simple piste map right in front of your eyes. Linked to an audio component, it also speaks to guide you to the nearest half-pipe, terrain park or mountain restaurant. And there's no danger of getting lost off-piste; it even issues an audible warning when you're about to leave a marked trail. So no more excuses!*

224

## 52

# Love your hardware

**Wax it, screw it, align it. Looking after your hardware may sound kinky, but it really will appreciate your loving touch.**

Learn how to give your kit this loving touch and you'll save money, ride better and learn a lot more about how your pride and joy actually works. Ready for a bit of self-service?

Up until a few years ago I never gave any thought to looking after my snowboard. OK, so there would be a few days after buying it when I'd turn into a paranoid parent over how my precious new stick was stored, but invariably by the end of the week I'd be chucking it on the back of the shuttle bus with everyone else's and clearing it into a cold cupboard at the end of the hols.

Then came my wake-up call. After six months in a dark dusty den, I hauled it out to pack for my next trip only to find the edges covered in rust. Since then I get it serviced more often than my car.

## IT PAYS TO PREPARE, PROTECT AND PRESERVE

Although it's much easier to simply stick your skis or snowboard into your local snow shop for a service, it's far cheaper (and actually quite simple) to do it yourself.

Start by filing those edges for a faster and more responsive ride. With a snowboard, pick an edge and draw an edge file down using sharp, short strokes. Use the file's own weight to sharpen the edge and don't force it. Do the same for each edge on both rails (sides).

*Here's an idea for you...*

**Just bought a new board or pair of skis? Don't wait until you've ridden the wax off them – start smearing as soon as you know when and where you're going to be riding. As well as making you go faster, waxing a brand new board or skis will also protect them.**

Filing the edges of skis is a slightly more precise art and it's a good idea to get some advice from your local technician first, as different parts of the ski should be filed depending on the effect you want. Once you and the technician have worked out where you need to file, you'll need a 'world cup file' or a 'Toko precision file guide' that sets the correct angles when filing.

Now you'll slice through anything, how about getting a bit of speed to your sticks too? Get out the wax. There are dozens of different waxes designed for every possible snow condition. Try to hold off on waxing until you know the type of conditions you'll be riding in next.

Place your board or skis base side up on a flat surface. Heat an old iron to a low setting and run it over the base. Then point the nose of the iron down and melt the wax onto your base. As the wax hits the base, it will cool and set quickly. Once you have a good covering, use the iron to spread the wax all over the base until it is covered. Let the heat of the iron work the wax into the base, but feel the underside (top sheet) to make sure it doesn't get too hot. If it's uncomfortable to touch, stop and let it cool.

**It's not just your gear that needs protecting – your body will benefit too. Turn to Idea 12, *The best defence*, and practise a bit of self-defence.**

*Try another idea...*

Once the wax has set, get a scraper and scrape the wax off using strong downward strokes from nose to tail until any excess wax flakes off.

Finally, don't forget your boots. Before stashing these at the end of the season, make sure they are thoroughly dry.

This means taking out your liners, but don't place them on hot radiators, because most liners are constructed using thermo-mouldable materials that have already adapted to the shape of your feet. A hot radiator will ruin this.

To store your ski boots, reinsert the liner. Once both parts of the boot are dry, reinsert, positioning the tongue correctly, as if you were skiing. Close the buckles to the same ratchet position that you ski in to maintain the correct shape of the boot.

Pick a place that's cool and dry to store all your snowsports gear. Heat will distort the shape of ski and snowboard, boots and liners, and breaks down the composition of a ski boot's plastic shell making it brittle.

*'A stitch in time saves nine.'*
Annoyingly accurate English proverb.

*Defining idea...*

*How did it go?*

**Q** **I've packed up my skis until next season. Should I get them serviced before stashing them in the attic, or is best to wait until just before my next trip?**

*A* *At the end of the season, get a close-down service where wax isn't scraped off, thereby protecting the base and edges. At the start of the season the technician will 'open them up', normally at no cost.*

*A professional service every now and then will also help maintain the structure of a ski's base by running it through a stone grinding machine. Too often will wear the base, but it needs to be done at least once a year.*

**Q** **Do I need to tune up my snowboard for riding rails?**

*A* *Catch an edge on a metal rail and you'll know about it. That's why many pros who ride rails actually blunt and 'detune' their edges as much as possible. If you don't do this, you'll find the edges will catch mid-rail, making it a bit of a roller-coaster ride.*

*To detune your board, place it on the floor and mark where the four corners touch the floor. Then file about an inch either side of the mark so that it is no longer sharp. See how this works for you, but remember that you're the only one who can judge how your board feels when you ride it sharp and in top tune. So get servicing and find out what suits your style best.*

# The end...

Or is it a new beginning?

We hope that you've been inspired to try a few new things to make your next snow experience the best yet. We hope that you're already getting more out of your time on the slopes by making small changes to your equipment, diet, planning and technique.

So why not let us know about it? Tell us how you got on. What did it for you – what really got you leaping out of bed to start your day on the mountain. Maybe you've got some tips of your own that you want to share (see the next page if so). And if you liked this book you may find we have more brilliant ideas for other areas that could help change your life for the better.

You'll find the Infinite Ideas crew waiting for you online at www.infideas.com.

Or if you prefer to write, then send your letters to:
*Skiing & snowboarding*
The Infinite Ideas Company Ltd
36 St Giles, Oxford, OX1 3LD, United Kingdom

We want to know what you think, because we're all working on making our lives better too. Give us your feedback and you could win a copy of another *52 Brilliant Ideas* book of your choice. Or maybe get a crack at writing your own.

Good luck. Be brilliant.

# Offer one

## CASH IN YOUR IDEAS

We hope you enjoy this book. We hope it inspires, amuses, educates and entertains you. But we don't assume that you're a novice, or that this is the first book that you've bought on the subject. You've got ideas of your own. Maybe our author has missed an idea that you use successfully. If so, why not put it in an email and send it to: yourauthormissedatrick@infideas.com, and if we like it we'll post it on our bulletin board. Better still, if your idea makes it into print we'll send you four books of your choice. or the cash equivalent. You'll be fully credited so that everyone knows you've had another Brilliant Idea.

# Offer two

## HOW COULD YOU REFUSE?

Amazing discounts on bulk quantities of Infinite Ideas books are available to corporations, professional associations and other organisations.

For details call us on:
+44 (0)1865 514888
fax: +44 (0)1865 514777
or e-mail: info@infideas.com

# Where it's at ...

## Win at the gym

Steve Shipside

*"I was so out of shape and overweight that my doctor told me I was well on my way to chronic back pain. I would have answered back but I was fully engaged in sucking in my belly at the time. I'm no superman and I was never a natural gym bunny yet now I'm an Iron Man triathlete and ultrarunner. That's despite having Better Things To Do (watching telly, washing up, anything really).*

*On the way I've learnt that there is no marathon as grim and as glum as getting nowhere in the gym. If you've ever caught a glimpse of yourself in the gym mirrors and thought, 'What's the point?', then these are the ideas you need to go the distance, and get the results you want."*
– **Steve Shipside**

**Available
from all good bookshops
or call us on
+44 (0) 1865 514888**

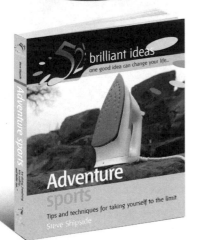

## Adventure sports

Steve Shipside

*"Remember when marathons were something only a few extraordinary athletes did? Now your neighbour's done one. In a rhino costume. The same is happening across the board as people of all ages realise that paragliding, white water rafting, abseiling, ultra running, wakeboarding and the rest are all entirely possible (and enormous fun) for us mere mortals.*

*Increasingly fringe sports are being sought out not just by thrill seekers, but by those who may have never felt comfortable in traditional sports. Or just those who have never felt comfortable being stereotyped. There is almost no limit to the variety on offer or the different degrees of thrills and risks. This book takes a look at the vast range of adventure sports now on offer and how you can master them while turning up the adrenaline volume in the process."* – **Steve Shipside**

## Re-energise your sex life
Elisabeth Wilson

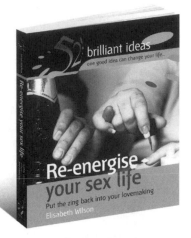

*"Sex manuals. They're either full of photos of impossibly lithesome twenty-somethings doing it in a state of almost clinical cleanliness or line drawings of men with beards who look like they're straight out of a Bee Gees tribute band."*

*"Well, this isn't a sex manual. You won't find any pictures in here. What you will find is inspirational ideas for people who've lost a little of that zing. So if you and your partner are in a bit of a rut, too tired from work or from looking after the kids to even feign headaches let alone orgasms, then I can help!"* – **Elisabeth Wilson**

**Available from all good bookshops or call us on +44 (0) 1865 514888**

## Look gorgeous always
Linda Bird

*"Looking beautiful is about much more than possessing fantastic cheek-bones and endless legs, though of course, great genes do help. The good news is that vitality, confidence, a savvy wardrobe, a few great make up and grooming tricks can work wonders too."*

*"The trick is to look after yourself, and to learn how to use what you've got to your best advantage. It's about maximising your beautiful bits, minimising the less beautiful ones, and faking a few more. "*

*"Look gorgeous always will help you unlock the ravishing creature that lies within. It provides lots of simple but ingenious tips that that I've learned from the leading lights in health and beauty. Try these brilliant ideas today – and feel more gorgeous, instantly!"* – **Linda Bird**

237

## Perfect parties

Lizzie O'Prey

*"Do you panic when you have to plan a formal dinner party? Is the thought of arranging a birthday bash enough to bring you out in a rash? If you've always wanted to be able to plan and prepare the perfect event then this is the place to start. From casual cocktails when you want to relax with friends to formal dining that is part and parcel of your job, you'll quickly see that there is an easy way to plan the affair.*

*Whether I've been planning a wedding or arranging an office party, speaking at a corporate event or having dinner with people I've never met before (and, aside from work, may never meet again), I have always approached any form of entertaining with one thing in mind. People should be relaxed. I've learned how to achieve that in both work and social situations and the practical tips and guide to planning events in this book can help you to achieve it too."* – **Lizzie O'Prey**

## Live longer

Sally Brown

*"You can live a long and healthy life. Amazingly, anti-ageing scientists believe that only 1 in 10,000 people die of old age. The vast majority of us die prematurely from what we've come to call 'natural causes'. In fact, cell structure studies show that biologically our true lifespan is between 110 and 120 years!*

*All the advice you'll find in Live longer is achievable and can be fun too! Some of the best anti-ageing strategies involve having sex, drinking red wine and spending time with friends. So, live long and enjoy!"* – **Sally Brown**